Writing Still Matters

I0894167

Writing Still Matters

Improving Student Writing in an Age of AI and Beyond

**Kristen Hawley Turner, Tanya Baker,
Elyse Eidman-Aadahl,
and Tonya B. Perry**

Teachers College Press
Teachers College, Columbia University

1234 Amsterdam Avenue
New York, NY 10027

national writing project

2120 UNIVERSITY AVE,
BERKELEY, CA 94704

Co-published by Teachers College Press, 1234 Amsterdam Avenue, New York, NY 10027 and National Writing Project (NWP), a fiscally sponsored project of Community Initiatives.

Front cover design by Geronna Lewis-Lyte. Image by Marissa Grootes / Unsplash.

Library of Congress Cataloging-in-Publication Data

Names: Turner, Kristen Hawley author | Baker, Tanya author | Eidman-Aadhal, Elyse author | Perry, Tonya B. author
Title: Writing still matters : improving student writing in an age of AI and beyond / Kristen Hawley Turner, Tanya Baker, Elyse Eidman-Aadhal, and Tonya B. Perry.
Description: New York, NY : Teachers College Press, [2026] | Includes bibliographical references and index. | Summary: "Translates longstanding National Writing Project (NWP) principles for a field being reshaped by AI. Includes classroom examples and teaching strategies for K-12 classrooms"—Provided by publisher.
Identifiers: LCCN 2026017617 (print) | LCCN 2026017618 (ebook) | ISBN 9780807784419 paperback | ISBN 9780807784587 hardcover | ISBN 9780807784594 ebook
Subjects: LCSH: English language—Composition and exercises—Study and teaching | Artificial intelligence—Educational applications
Classification: LCC LB1576 .T89 2026 (print) | LCC LB1576 (ebook)
LC record available at https://lccn.loc.gov/2026017617
LC ebook record available at https://lccn.loc.gov/2026017618

ISBN 978-0-8077-8441-9 (paper)
ISBN 978-0-8077-8458-7 (hardcover)
ISBN 978-0-8077-8459-4 (ebook)

Printed on acid-free paper

Manufactured in the United States of America

We dedicate this book to the Teacher Consultants in the National Writing Project, who for over 50 years have continued to learn, collaborate, share, lead, advocate, and, most importantly of all, write.

Contents

Authors' Note

In the process of writing a book that touches on the teaching of writing in the age of AI, we knew we needed to grapple with and argue about the role of AI in our own writing as a way to question the role of generative AI (GenAI) in the work of writers more broadly. Over time, our individual and collective views shifted through our conversations with one another and with educators throughout our networks. Ultimately, our experimentation with GenAI tools and our steadfast beliefs about the importance of the human writer in a process of making meaning taught us much.

Various GenAI tools were used throughout the preparation of this manuscript. GenAI served as a thinking partner to help us organize and develop our argument, a research assistant to curate and summarize literature and data, and a co-writer to refine chapters and develop profiles. GenAI was a collaborator along the way, and the result is the culmination of our collective thinking. As humans, however, we always claimed agency in the process, and the final words you are reading throughout this book are the ones that we, the authorial team, put on the page.

PREFACE

A Brief History of the National Writing Project

Writing has been called "the forgotten R," as reading and 'rithmatic often steal center stage in discussions about education. But sometimes attention to writing seems to capture national attention.

So it was in 1974 when a small group of teachers and professors in the San Francisco Bay Area were gathered together by faculty member James Gray at the University of California, Berkeley, to spend the summer examining the teaching of writing across secondary and university classrooms. Motivated by the poor showing of students on UC Berkeley's mandatory placement exam in writing, university administrators had agreed to sponsor a "fellowship program" for these educators, each recognized as a strong and effective teacher of writing. The "Summer Fellows," as they came to be called, used their summer to demonstrate their most promising approaches to teaching writing, dive into the growing research on writing, and explore the practice of writing by writing themselves. After their summer program, these Summer Fellows became "Teacher Consultants," subsequently working with their colleagues to lead efforts to improve the teaching of writing back in their schools and institutions, expanding their focus to all grades and subject areas. That summer and this new idea of "teachers teaching teachers" marked the start of the Bay Area Writing Project (BAWP), the founding site of what would become the National Writing Project (NWP).

There was something in the air about writing and teaching writing at that time as the nation's largest cohort of college-age students filled classrooms across the nation. In 1975, *Newsweek* published its (in)famous cover article, "Why Johnny Can't Write," sparking conversation about how writers are cultivated, and scholars such as Janet Emig and Donald Graves and writers such as Donald Murray surfaced the importance of process, as compared to a singular focus on product, in writing. As open admissions programs, such as the one at City University of New York, brought an expanded population of young people into higher education, scholars such as Mike Rose and Mina Shaughnessy powerfully advocated that professors dive into the practice of teaching *all* our nation's students how to write. The ability to write clearly and thoughtfully was understood to be linked to advancement in college and career, and if the nation was serious about expanding opportunities to the widest range of young people, instruction in writing would need to be a focus, not just in first-year composition programs for already accepted students, but throughout K–12 education. Writing mattered, not just for the few, but for the many.

With a view toward the many, the moment was ripe for the idea of a writing project like the one in the Bay Area to spread across the nation. By the end of the decade, seven new writing projects had grown up at universities around the country. Over time, the numbers continued to grow, with hundreds of thousands of teachers and professors participating in leadership and professional development programs launched in all 50 states; Washington, DC; Puerto Rico; and the U.S. Virgin Islands. In 1991, a formal network called the National Writing Project was established to support these local projects and link teacher leaders and scholars across the nation for colleagueship and shared work.

In subsequent years, a rich field of writing studies emerged in graduate programs around the country, and new curricula were developed and evaluated, pointing to a wide range of effective practices in teaching writing. Many of the graduates of those programs would go on to found local writing project sites at their universities and to create research programs that involved K–12 classroom teachers as equal partners. Teachers and scholars began to shape large-scale assessment programs such as the National Assessment of Educational Progress to take up the challenge of illuminating what students knew and were able to do in writing. Others conducted basic research into the practice of writing across developmental stages and within diverse communities.

Increasingly, teachers and scholars at local writing project sites used their common network to mount national projects focused on the shared challenges that research and assessment made visible. An Urban Sites Network and a Rural Sites Network formed to work on teaching writing in the inequitable conditions of inner-city and rural schools. Groups focused on teaching writing to students learning English, improving the teaching of academic writing, examining civic argument, and theorizing the impact of new technologies on writing and connected learning, each developed organically in response to the time and identified needs of writers and teachers of writing. Throughout, NWP sites continued to refine their ways of working to produce and examine new knowledge, focusing on models of inquiry and learning from practice in diverse communities that always included teacher leaders as full participants.

As a network, the National Writing Project has been shaped by and contributed to the growing body of theory and research related to writing and writing instruction. The Teacher Consultants who participate in NWP institutes, conduct inquiry into their practice, and share their knowledge with others form the core of the network. They are connected through local sites and national initiatives. They are passionate about developing writers and improving the state of writing instruction. They embrace opportunities for professional learning. These qualities are the essence of NWP.

In the 50 years following that first summer institute at the University of California, Berkeley, this community of educators and colleagues has created a rich legacy of knowledge and practice about writing and the teaching of writing. NWP has learned much about how writing shapes thinking, how communities shape writers, and how identity shapes the experience of writing. However, the job of improving the teaching of writing for the many, and not just the few, is not done.

In the winter of 2025, in the 51st year of the history of the National Writing Project, 3 years after ChatGPT entered conversations about teaching writing in schools, the time felt ripe for NWP to share what we know about the teaching of writing *now*, not because our knowledge is complete and there is nothing left to learn, but because we want to proclaim loudly, against any voice that might say otherwise, that *Writing Still Matters*, maybe more than it ever has. We are, it seems, at another inflection point. This book captures this moment in time, an era that has been built on decades of research and practice even as technologies impact what writing is, what writers do, and how writing teachers must adapt to continue the work of the NWP.

Writing Still Matters

Introduction

This book is authored by four writers who have spent decades learning with and through the educators in the National Writing Project network. The landscape for writing and writing instruction has changed over their careers as new research emerged, as assessment and policy reshaped schools, and as new technologies changed the way writers create and circulate their writing. In January 2024, months after ChatGPT made its debut into public consciousness, one member of this writing team was attending a conference hosted by the Institute of Education Sciences (IES), an office of the U.S. Department of Education, where a senior official in the department gave a keynote address, proclaiming, "Perhaps we won't even need to teach writing in the future, now that we all have access to ChatGPT."

This book is meant to be an argument against that idea. In fact, contrary to that assertion, this book argues that with ever more powerful tools, the teaching of writing is more important than ever.

This is not the first time that NWP has taken a stand in support of writing. In 2003, members of the NWP network worked with writer Carl Nagin to sum up knowledge and perspectives that characterized the field of writing in a book titled *Because Writing Matters* (2003). Published at a time of widespread emphasis on standards, assessment, and disparities in achievement and marked by the passage in early 2002 of No Child Left Behind, *Because Writing Matters* advocated improvements in curriculum, practice, and professional development that would increase achievement in writing, particularly in the context of new higher-stakes assessments. However, its publication preceded the dramatic changes in digital technologies and broad internet connectivity that would transform environments and expectations for writing.

By 2010, digital tools and internet connectivity had made such a significant impact on the basic ecosystem of written communication that NWP published a second text, *Because Digital Writing Matters* (NWP et al., 2010), to argue that digital composing, internet connectivity, and connected learning both inside and outside of schools would reshape writing and writing instruction in the 21st century. And indeed they have. In the time following *Because Digital Writing Matters,* online composing and digital circulation have become ubiquitous and routine. Writing and writing instruction take place in interconnected writing environments, on social media, and in interactive or game-based environments. Students at ever younger ages participate in digital spaces with both positive and negative results. Writing itself is ever more fully multimodal, blending visual, auditory, graphic, and performative elements more geared to circulation via screens than paper.

The current era marks another moment of transformation as new generative AI models raise questions about what it means to write and to be an author in environments that include intelligent, though not strictly human, agents. Readers and writers persist amidst a sea of mis- and disinformation that is getting ever more sophisticated in its design and operation, easily outstripping the speed of curriculum development and educational change. Yet new questions, whether about educational systems, new technologies, or emerging social and civic challenges, inevitably sit alongside the deeply human experience of writing.

Writing is still one of the most powerful tools humans have created for thinking, communicating, experiencing, and shaping community; managing joint action; and realizing new social possibilities. Through writing, each individual, embedded in communities, cultures, and histories, puts themselves, their thoughts, and their stories out into the world. When educators understand that power, it changes everything. Writing still matters—arguably more than ever.

When everybody writes and software can contribute output, teaching writing wisely and well matters. As authors of this new book in the tradition of *Because Writing Matters* and *Because Digital Writing Matters,* we are members of the community of educators who are the National Writing Project. This work reflects 50 years of research, rich conversations, and deeply held beliefs across the NWP network about writing and the teaching of writing. Building on the previous books, we draw on and share the experience and knowledge of the many colleagues, researchers, and teachers who have shaped the National Writing Project into what it is today. In this book, we examine core questions of practice for teachers of writing: Why and how does writing matter, and how does that answer inform our practice? How should we focus on writing at all grade levels and across subject areas? How can we honor both the writer and a community of writers? Where do new technologies fit into writing instruction? We also hope to express what NWP has learned about professional development and teacher leadership, two of our signature activities.

Finally, much like the authors of *Because Writing Matters* and *Because Digital Writing Matters*, we are motivated to engage the knowledge and principles of NWP with the issues and questions that are facing teachers now. The book consists of focused chapters that draw on the lessons of the previous two editions while layering in new knowledge and considering the moment in which we live.

In Chapter 1, we address what writing is and why it matters. Building on the core assertion of *Because Writing Matters*, that writing is complex, we take a closer look at what it means to "be a writer"—the basic identity we hope to cultivate in our students. At its most denotative level, of course, "writers are people who write," but we argue there is more to inhabiting the identity of "a writer" than just producing text. Together, these beliefs about writing and being a writer represent ideas that have been foundational to NWP and our model of professional learning and teacher leadership. From them, we draw implications for teaching writing. The implications sound simple, but they can be challenging to put into practice.

In Chapter 2, we examine some of the myths that continue to persist in writing instruction, limiting teachers' ability to adopt effective practices. We provide a summary of the research that refutes those myths, along with examples drawn from teachers we have known and worked with who have pushed their instruction to match what they know about how writing is best taught and learned.

Chapter 3 takes up the challenge of new technologies—a challenge so significant to our practices today that it deserves its own chapter. We build on the argument in *Because Digital Writing Matters* to include issues that have emerged since its publication, including the opportunity for multimodal composition, the challenges around research and digital citizenship, and the promise and peril of generative AI and writing assistance tools in the classroom. We have strived to consider and incorporate voices and practices of students who may sometimes be left out of the conversation around new technologies.

Chapter 4 brings many of these themes together as we look at the opportunities to expand our understanding of writing and the teaching of writing beyond classroom walls. Growing from our foundational beliefs about how writing connects us to the world and can be supercharged by the affordances of digital tools and internet technologies, we look at writing through the lens of connected learning and civic engagement. The role of writing and rhetoric in democratic civic life is well established, but more recently NWP leaders have expanded their thinking about how writing and civic life intersect and how classrooms can create a context for learning to write that has special power.

In Chapter 5, we return to lessons learned about teacher leadership and professional learning over the 50 years of NWP work. In an age of GenAI, how can teachers learn and lead? We look at professional development, teachers as writers, and the potential for teachers to create community for their students and themselves. At its core, this chapter is an invitation for readers to learn with us.

We end with a coda that looks to the writing classroom of the future. We highlight the possibilities of the integration of AI in classrooms of tomorrow and the collaborative work that can be generated when AI is a tool that students and teachers use, leading to increased productivity and critical analyses "because writing matters."

Throughout this book, we aim to honor the first 50 years of the National Writing Project and look forward with hope and expectation to the next 50 years. Each of us on the writing team and most of those quoted in the book have been teachers of writing. We know well the special excitement of a lively writing classroom, crackling with the energy of young people discovering new ideas and expressing themselves. We've seen students of all types and circumstances come alive with the sense of authority that authorship conveys. Writing matters for many reasons: for advancement in college and career, for the advancement of knowledge, and for democratic civic life. As teachers, though, we say writing matters because *writers* matter, which is to say that our students matter, all of them. It is with student writers in mind that we tackle the question of why writing *still* matters.

CHAPTER 1

Writing and Writers

NWP Core Principles

Writing is still essential for human connection and communication.
—Pauline Schmidt, West Chester University

> My students may come into my class hating to write, but many of them leave knowing that their words matter. Through authentic daily writing, we reveal the beauty of the world and the wonder of ourselves. We reveal the truths and tragedies of our history. And we unleash our hopes and dreams. Writing matters because no one else can or should tell our stories. They are ours to share. And the more clearly and beautifully we can tell our stories, the more we will understand each other and heal our world.
>
> —Cindy Jenson-Elliott, Madison High School and UCSD Extended Studies

Writing still matters because it is our primary way of presenting our identity to the world, whether that be through a text message, an email, a college application essay, a report at our job, a holiday letter, or prompts engineered to get what we want from Artificial Intelligence platforms. . . . What really matters about writing today is not the product on a page or screen, but the transformation created in our brains and hearts.
—Kel Sassi, Northern Michigan University

> It's where I really know what I know. It's where I can clarify my own thoughts to see where I stand on a matter. It's where I discover who I am.
>
> —Kristen Glenn, Brigham Young University

Anyone who has ever composed a joke or story that made someone laugh out loud, written a poem that contained a metaphor that caused the reader to gasp, or crafted an argument that changed someone's mind knows that writing is powerful. In fact, it is something close to magic. Writing makes thinking visible, transforming something inside one person's mind into an artifact to be consumed, processed, and acted upon. Writing allows humans to uncover what they are thinking and to share it with others across the reaches of time and space.

Perhaps because of the magic underlying writing, it is also incredibly complex. It is a product—an essay, a novel, a multimedia presentation—and it is also a process that people engage in to create a particular product, for a particular purpose, in a particular context. At its best, writing is both cognitive and social, an opportunity to communicate and also to inquire, explore ideas, and ultimately come to understand oneself more deeply.

For over 50 years, scholars and practitioners in the National Writing Project (NWP) have worked together to unpack the magic of writing in all its complexity—doing it, teaching it, studying it—uncovering nuances about what writing is and what writers do in order to share the practices that honor writer identities and the author's craft. Over 5 decades, the NWP network has honed these practices into a set of core principles that guide the understanding of how teachers of writing can cultivate writers and also can continue to learn and grow across their careers as writing, technologies, and contexts change.

This chapter provides a way to think about what writing is, what writers do, and how writers grow. It includes a brief history of the research that undergirds the field's understanding of teaching writing, as well as the core principles that guide National Writing Project's work on improving the teaching of writing.

WHAT WRITING IS

From the outside looking in, writing can appear to be simple transcription, moving sentences from the mind to an external space—paper, screen, or otherwise. But inside, people who write understand writing as a complex mental task. It involves retrieval of information or memories, yes, but retrieval is just the beginning. Writers then have to plan and make decisions about what to include and what to leave out, what order to put things in, and what style of language and turns of phrase—and perhaps what media—work best to convey their ideas to their intended audiences.

Research confirms that this complexity of language work rewires the brain. It supports memory consolidation, moving experience and new information from short-term to long-term memory. The very act of writing helps to regulate emotions around difficult memories and situations, as well as complex ideas or topics. Writing offers humans capacity as a tool for communication, and it also helps to better understand human experience. In other words, writing is a form of thinking and meaning-making that can stretch an individual and the collective (Johnston, 2025). Cognitive psychologists have coined the term "desirable difficulties" (Bjork, 1994, p. 193) to describe acts like writing that make learning or practice just the right level of difficult, one that is often more frustrating in the short term, but ultimately more effective in the long run as learners engage with something at the edge of their reach.

While much of the history of writing across time is a history of inventing new tools and practices to make the task of writing easier and more efficient, making the production of writing less challenging, writers still need to value the stretch. But in an age of generative AI, writers and teachers of writers find themselves in an area of steep learning as humans sort out what is desirable difficulty (Epstein, 2025), or, as researchers at West Ed have called it, "friction by design" (WestEd, 2025), and what is difficulty that just gets in the way. Or said another way, "What are writers outsourcing that they should be doing for themselves?"

One way to answer this question is to think about what writers do that improves their capacities and their lives in the long run. In other words, how does writing improve the writer?

WHAT WRITERS DO

Researchers who study how writing rewires the brain point to how the act of writing engages the prefrontal cortex, the part of the brain related to goal-setting and problem-solving. Even something as simple as writing a list supports the development of this part of the brain. It also happens when writers make connections between complicated ideas and move experiences or new knowledge into deeper understanding. Additionally, it can work as a coolant for human emotions. When writers write about their feelings or emotional responses to stimuli, they gain emotional distance. The effect is to shift one's mental state from anxiety or other consuming emotions to more grounded clarity. All of these effects taken together build resilience in people who write.

Over the 50+ years of the National Writing Project, educators have come to understand that writing is something that can hit that magic level of "desirable difficulty." Teachers must think about how to best support students' growth as people—people who write. And, as teachers explore how to integrate AI into their classroom writing practices, this charge is no less true.

The arrival of generative AI means that, as always, educators have much to learn about teaching writing at this moment. Teachers can and will engage with the implications of this new technology. But at the same time, the human dimensions of writing to learn, writing to find and express meaning, and writing to communicate are as relevant today as they have ever been. The challenge of this moment, of course, is to consider how GenAI can be a part of that.

A BRIEF HISTORY OF RESEARCH INTO WRITING AND THE TEACHING OF WRITING

Though current understandings of writing accept that it is both process and product, this was not always the case. As chronicled in *Because Writing Matters,* until the 1970s writing instruction generally addressed writing as a product. Researchers like Janet Emig, Donald Murray, and Peter Elbow opened new ways of thinking about writing that began to center the writer as a person engaged in a process of writing. Cognitive theorists such as Linda Flower and John Hayes explored the process within the writer's mind, while a sociocultural view sparked by Lev Vygotsky's work pushed the field to understand that writers and their texts do not exist in isolation. Writers are influenced by and contribute to broader cultural and social contexts, and they are often composing for readers. Later scholars such as Arnetha Ball and Jacqueline Jones Royster expanded this view to take account of the specific experiences of youth of color, surfacing particular traditions for literacy learning in their communities.

In the 1970s, student writers were increasingly seen as culturally and linguistically rich, creating ideas, words, and thoughts that came from a place of textured heritage and respected language.

Researchers like Geneva Smitherman and Victor Villanueva wrote about the importance of respect for students' languages and allowing space for them to convey their ideas without fear of rejection for use of their own dialect and language patterns. Luis Moll showed how the core cultural practices and bodies of knowledge that are embedded in the daily practices and routines of families could serve as funds of knowledge for improving writing and learning more generally. This understanding shifted practice from viewing the teacher as the only expert with language to the students also having language agency. It also led to a better understanding of the multiple languages and dialects that exist in classrooms, as well as the beauty of the variation.

By the 1980s, there was general agreement in the field that focusing instruction only on the product of writing—by asking students to write to a task and submit a single draft—might produce a better product at each instance, yet still fail to improve students' overall capacity as writers. In other instances, scholars such as Mina Shaughnessy and Mike Rose documented how such practices could actually stymie developing writers. Influenced by cognitive and sociocognitive approaches to learning and development advanced by researchers such as Jean Piaget, Bärbel Inhelder, and Lev Vygotsky, teachers and scholars such as Donald Graves, Anne Haas Dyson, and Sarah Freedman explored *processes* of composition at different ages. From research at this time, which included the close observation of writers at work, the field identified phases and activities in the act of writing—planning, conceptualizing, drafting, revising, and editing. Scholars also began to focus on writing as a communicative act, seeing how writers worked to imagine both purpose and audiences for what they produced.

A sociocultural view of writing as a process influenced a dramatic shift in how writing was taught. Thought leaders like Nancie Atwell and Lucy Calkins promoted writing workshop approaches that cultivated individual writers in a community of other writers, treating the classroom as a workshop where student writers engaged in the act of writing as artists or craftspeople might in their workshops. Pedagogies that included writing workshop models allowed student writers to have real audiences that were not just the teacher. Peers provided feedback, support, and response throughout a writer's process.

Similarly, the sociocultural emphasis on how writing is embedded in discourse communities sparked rich work in how writing was understood across the curriculum, where practitioners in various disciplines began to look carefully at how the writing they do and the writing they require from students functions within the larger context of the disciplines they teach. Ernest Morrell's work centered student thinking as writers learned to use their writing to impact across disciplines and in larger spaces beyond the classroom.

Eventually, the advent of digital technologies and the read-write web opened the possibilities of purposes, audiences, and contexts well beyond the classroom. Writing in today's world is digital, multimodal, and networked, influenced heavily by the technologies available to writers. The New London Group led the way in thinking about "new literacies," and theorists like Gunther Kress helped expand understandings of multimodality. The research around and through the "digital turn" (Mills, 2010) inspired new thinking about what writing is and what writers do, with specific attention to the context of the internet, where writers could share their thinking relatively easily and be connected to a community of readers and writers through their screens.

The advent of online writing as participation by an individual in a community led researchers such as Jean Lave and Etienne Wenger to try to understand how humans are shaped by the communities in which they participate. Digital writing allowed individuals to exert agency in the world, and in more recent research by the Connected Learning Network, Mimi Ito and colleagues explored writing for individual growth and opportunities as well as civic engagement, pushing the field to understand the value of passion, purpose, and action in a writer's participation within communities of writers.

When *Because Digital Writing Matters* was published in 2010, researchers and teachers were extraordinarily optimistic about the power of digital, interconnected writing to lift voices and share both individual and collective experiences. In the intervening years, a more complicated and nuanced picture has emerged. While the world has seen the power of digital writing, it has also seen the consequences of unfettered publication, including widespread mis- and disinformation, the proliferation of hateful and disturbing rhetoric, and a rise in adolescent depression and anxiety that scholars like Jonathan Haidt, in the *Anxious Generation* (2024), have blamed on the use of social media.

As new forms of technology arise, most especially generative artificial intelligence based on large language models (LLMs), the impact on writing—both the process and the product—remains to be seen. Technologies have the potential to make writing more efficient, but at the same time they may transform writing practices. Regardless of the impact, writing must continue to be the result of productive struggle, the desirable difficulty that engages writers in what they know, believe, and want to say.

It is because of the ability to write and publish writing to large audiences and because of the capacity of that writing to impact, in ways beautiful and good, as well as ways dark and bad, that writing and the teaching of writing still matter, maybe more than ever. Over the last 50 years, a changing understanding of writing and writers has been reflected in university-based research and emerging theoretical conceptions of the writing process. At the same time, teachers themselves, especially those with National Writing Project experience, have developed and tested pedagogical applications. Practitioners have formulated new ways to teach writing, taken up and taught the use of digital tools, developed individual writers' identities and decision-making capacities, and ushered students into communities of writers with a focus on ethical participation in those spaces.

Finally, although these different threads of modern writing research might seem to be markedly different, they are perhaps better understood as layers of insight on a foundation that has consistently examined three questions:

What is writing, and what is effective writing?
What are writers doing when they produce writing?
How can people learn to write better?

Although these questions have occupied scholars of rhetoric for millennia, scientific knowledge about these questions constitutes a rich and growing body of work that has been reviewed and iterated over the last half-century. Knowledge about writing and the teaching of writing is not a "single thing," as phrases like "the science of writing" might suggest. Rather, it has a long history, coupled with rapid changes in technologies. The study of writing instruction is complex and draws on cognitive science, sociocultural theory, digital media studies, and critical pedagogy to understand how people write and learn to create in a rapidly changing world. Yet despite its complexity, the scientific body of research is remarkably coherent, as are the implications for teaching writing. When synthesized, the research reveals what might be called "core principles."

IMPLICATIONS FOR THE TEACHING OF WRITING: NWP CORE PRINCIPLES

As participants in and contributors to the sweep of research described in this chapter, NWP has drawn a small number of general implications for the improvement of practice in the teaching of writing. These were the focus of NWP's earlier books, *Because Writing Matters* in 2003 and *Because Digital Writing Matters* in 2010, and they still ring true today.

Writing Can and Should Be Taught (Not Just Assigned) at All Grade Levels

Teaching writing, rather than simply assigning and then grading it, offers an opportunity to see students' thinking through a process of feedback, conversation, and revision. From this process, teachers gain clarity for future lessons, both individualized and whole-class. This visible thinking can help teachers decide which direction to go and how to get there with students.

Teachers focused on the process of writing help students learn how to select and limit topics, organize their thinking, and work toward a polished finished product. A focus on process, by professional writers and student writers, makes visible the importance of productive struggle, the idea that "the very difficulty of writing is its virtue: it requires that students move beyond rote learning and simply reproducing information" (NWP, 2003, p. 23).

In the years since the publication of *Because Writing Matters*, new understandings of the relationship between learning and identity development have also expanded the focus of teaching writing from the process of producing writing to a focus on what it takes to develop students' writerly identities. Understanding that human beings have multiple identities that impact one another and that learning often involves the development of a new identity, educators then must also understand that the new identities a student might embrace and believe in have much to do with social context—families, communities, schools, and how they interact with one another. While writing teachers may believe that "anyone who writes is a writer," students may be asking themselves, "*Can I be a writer?* Do I see or hear any writers who look like me? Talk like me? Come from the place that I come from?" Writing instructors focusing on identity development see and treat students as developing writers.

Whitney and Johnson (2017) described the difference between a "student," conforming to technical standards, and a "writer," creatively and agentively using tools and ideas to author an original work, this way:

> Whereas a student completes assignments, a writer composes texts. Where a student fulfills expectations, a writer makes decisions. Where a student writes well or poorly, or gets a good or bad grade, a writer communicates effectively or doesn't, persuades or doesn't, delights readers or doesn't. Writers are different from students in that writers develop and pursue agendas while students work within agendas set by others—as in standards documents or a teacher's lesson plans. (pp. 83–84)

While it is true that instruction can improve students' performance on writing assignments, for writing instruction to *make writers* it must be embedded in opportunities for those writers to make choices and feel ownership over their writing. Whereas in 2003 NWP wrote, "everyone can learn to write," today instructors are driven forward by the idea that "everyone is a writer."

Students Must Have the Opportunity to Explore Diverse Writing Tasks and to Make and Pursue Their Own Goals to Develop Competence and Confidence

In 2003 NWP argued that students need to engage with diverse writing tasks to develop competence, but that book did not project how the diversity of writing would evolve over the next 2 decades. Between the release of the Common Core State Standards in 2010 (National Governors Association Center for Best Practices & Council of Chief State School Officers), which emphasized teaching argument, and the growing awareness of the importance of genre overall, including forms of disciplinary, digital, and public writing, teaching students how to explore and analyze new forms of writing and approach unfamiliar tasks with confidence is essential.

And, of course, students today have the means to create and distribute compositions that are made of more than just words, creating multimodal content in all areas of their lives. As defined by Undarmaa Maamuujav et al. (2025):

> Multimodal content and texts combine both language (*words and sentences*) and other semiotic elements (*images, sound, symbols*) to construct meaning and deliver a message. As opposed to traditional, monomodal writing that solely uses linguistic (text-based) resources, writing multimodally involves design choices and purposeful integration of multiple modalities to mediate meaning-making. These choices are guided by several factors, including the domains and genres of writing, the rhetorical goals of the writer, the intended audience, and the communicative context. (p. 371)

Multimodality is more than simply adding decoration to a word-based text (Jewitt, 2006). Rather, it involves design thinking and problem-solving to consider how information presented in a number of modalities might work together as a single work. While students today may not see this kind of writing as having a place in school, teachers should aim to help students develop communication skills to do the work they want and need to do in the modern world.

Students Are Already Writers: Treat Them as Such

In 2010, NWP et al. argued that the "digital revolution" meant that many students come into the classroom as already published writers, even if they don't own that identity. Human lives are lived through writing—texts, social media posts, blogs, email, and fan fiction are just the tip of the iceberg of the way writing is a means of participation in society and in families and communities. And because of that, much of students' lived experience as writers stands in contrast to what teachers and schools might want to teach them or ask them to do. Their deep experience composing with text, as well as image, video, and sound, is a tremendous resource, but it is also a resource to be interrogated. In a life lived online, publication is instant, circulation is broad, and distant audiences can respond in seconds. Social media and group chats pressure individuals to write quickly and move on, with few opportunities for the careful consideration of complex ideas.

Teachers today understand that raising up writers in their classrooms has impacts outside of school. In a digital, interconnected world, it is not enough to make writers, focusing on the development of their individual identities, skills, capacities, and voices; teachers today also need to help individual writers adopt a responsible and ethical stance. Writing teachers today teach students how to check sources, use others' words responsibly and ethically, and give and receive feedback honestly. To participate in the public sphere through writing online is a form of civic learning (Kahne et al., 2016).

And so it may be that teaching students to sit in the productive struggle that moves their thinking forward and helps them to connect new learning to their currently held ideas, to be flexible and willing to change their minds in light of new information, to use writing as a tool to think, to think more deeply, and to rethink, may be more difficult than it was before. However, it is certainly more important than it has ever been. Today, teachers must take students seriously as writers and see it as part of the work of teaching writing to help young writers develop into ethical participants in writing communities.

AUTHORS' NOTE

You may have noticed a shift in voice from the Introduction to this chapter: from a personal lens to a more research-based lens. We did so intentionally and purposefully, although it took us a little while to finalize the decision. As writers and teachers of writing, our identities are shaped by these core principles of the National Writing Project. We feel so close to them, in fact, that much of our first-draft writing of this book included first-person reflections on what "we" have learned. We made the authorial decision to remove the royal "we" in order to look more broadly across the history of the network and the body of writing-related research that informs this book. At the same time, we know that "we," the four of us on the author team, have been shaped by all of the educators of NWP, and we want to acknowledge our individual and collective identities in these pages. This is the first of our reflective authors' notes where we give ourselves permission to speak from our view, encompassing, perhaps, a royal "we" that also includes you, the reader. We invite you to reflect alongside us each time we take this pause throughout the book.

CHAPTER 2

Persistent Myths About the Teaching of Writing

> Writing is for everyone, at every level of skill, from every background and lifestyle.
> —Jesus Vedoya Renteria, Hanaford West High School

Sometimes writing can begin as a list, a diagram, a map, a doodle, or another form of out-of-this-world holy wondering.
—Amy Estersohn, White Plains High School

> I have learned that telling an important story has very little to do with punctuation.
> —Star Friend, Dowel J. Howard High School

What I've learned about writing is how different the writing process looks for each student.
—S. J. Williamson, North Dakota State University

Chapter 1 argued that writing is a complex, high-level process of creative design and iterative making: one part creative and critical thinking, one part social awareness, and two parts patient hard work. Chapter 1 also outlined a history of knowledge-making through which the field has learned about writing and the teaching of writing as well as three NWP core principles that help guide teachers in planning for instruction. This chapter picks up from this background about writing itself to explore more about *teaching* such a complex, high-level endeavor.

In fact, for many teachers, knowledge of what the research says about writing and the teaching of writing has likely come in the context of pedagogical movements and new curricula informed by the research. Teachers' newfound attention to what writers actually *do* when they write, not just the forms they produce, became known as the process movement, a broad and catalytic movement that took on the aspiration that anyone and everyone could write and could improve their writing over time if they were taught to move through the processes of conceptualizing, drafting, revising, and publishing writing. In order to support young people to approach a wide range of written tasks with confidence and strategic planning, the process movement layered on the importance of choice, revision, audience, and authentic purpose. Then, as writing research matured and the social nature of writing came into sharper focus, teachers' practices took a "social turn." Careful ethnographic studies revealing how writing is not simply an individual act, but a social and cultural practice shaped by communities, identity, and power relationships, inspired teachers to take up practices that focused on creating communities of writers in their classrooms, emphasizing the collaborative nature of writing. They also became more cognizant of how writing foregrounds questions of identity and language variation in classrooms for both writers and their audiences.

Finally, throughout this period, the foundational tools that writers used to do their work exploded in a wave of digital innovation. By the turn of the 21st century, teachers were exploring the importance of "new literacies," beginning their own journeys with multimodal and digital writing, and raising questions—about equity, linguistic diversity, and technology's influence on writing practices and communities. As writing for the screen began to surpass writing for the page, the standardized forms and products that characterized older curricula were displaced by new forms of writing made possible by digital technologies and the internet. The impact on teaching practices continues as technologies like AI built on large language models have introduced a whole host of new questions for teachers and scholars alike.

Across the last 50 years, many schools and teachers working under the headings of the "process movement," writers workshop, writing across the curriculum, and the developing practices of multimodal and digital composition have drawn on the core principles outlined in Chapter 1 of having students learn to write in a way that is authentic to the practices that writers actually engage in, using the tools of real writers, in a community of developing writers. They have taught the specific skills that writers develop within the context of real writing tasks. The best news is that research has documented the success of these methods, as well as the nuances of practice that produce the most powerful results.

But one big puzzle remains. This body of research and practice has not, by and large, effected dramatic change in the way writing is taught in schools. Despite the many schools and classrooms where writing is taught well, there are many schools that have not yet created a strong writing program. Why is that?

We believe it comes down to a small set of myths, myths about how to teach writing that are deeply embedded in schooling, perpetuating practices that are reminiscent of a time before science, through empirical research, entered the field. These myths, which have a firm hold in classrooms and curricula, exist despite significant empirical evidence that disputes their effectiveness. In fact, these myths represent practices that need to be destabilized if writing teachers are to elevate the practices that pursue the goal of educating the broadest range of young people to become competent writers.

FIVE MYTHS THAT CONTINUE TO HAUNT THE TEACHING OF WRITING

Myth 1: Writing Is Transcription

Parents and teachers often tell the very youngest students that writing is "talk or thought written down." And in a way, that is true—the print code offers a powerful tool to freeze and mark ideas that would otherwise disappear into the ether. But the myth of transcription goes beyond that to suggest that learning to use the print code correctly is what the teaching of writing is all about.

This view of writing suggests that teaching spelling, punctuation, and grammar are the foundation, or the precursor, of writing. It leads to classroom practices that prioritize mechanics and grammar instruction in isolation as the first step in teaching writing. Teachers who hold this belief often assume that grammar mastery—or learning the rules—must come before "real writing." Or, in the earliest grades, they may delay having young people compose until students learn to read, positioning decoding as a prerequisite for production. As students mature, teachers might assume that learning to write a correct sentence comes before learning a correct paragraph, which then must precede the essay. When teachers treat writing primarily as transcription, they often focus on correctness rather than meaning-making, an approach that can reduce writing to error avoidance. As a result, students fail to develop the fluency that is necessary for them to generate and communicate ideas.

Scientific research reveals that transcription is just a small component of what writing is. Writing requires complex cognitive and rhetorical processes that include planning and goal-setting, idea generation and organization, drafting and revising, evaluating and anticipating audience response, and choosing appropriate modes and media for communicating meaning. Studies of young writers show that they can easily and enthusiastically begin to learn about generating ideas, setting goals, giving and receiving feedback, and anticipating audience reactions from the start, even as their transcription abilities grow. Research also demonstrates that the general understanding that all language users have the sense and syntax of their native language is a powerful resource for writing, even as they learn more about how to label and use the print code.

Helping students learn to write correctly is a valued goal. Yet as far back as the 1960s, research showed that traditional, isolated grammar instruction had no impact on writing ability and often did not even produce correctness. This finding has been confirmed over time, with the added insight that teaching grammar in isolation may negatively impact writing as students become risk-averse in their writing. Teaching grammar in context, with instruction connected to students' own drafts and the revision and editing process, can help students see grammar as a rhetorical tool, not just a set of rules, and this kind of instruction can positively impact writing ability.

Practices to Destabilize	Practices to Elevate
• Teaching grammar in isolation • Decoupling the teaching of reading and writing • Focusing grading on error correction	• Teaching grammar in context • Linking reading and writing instruction throughout the grades • Teaching students to generate ideas, set goals, and make a plan for writing from the beginning of literacy instruction

Myth-Busting NWP Teachers at Work

Because Tyler knows grammar instruction is best done within the context of writing, he plans to embed grammar instruction within the process of planning and goal-setting, generating ideas, drafting, revising, and editing.

He approaches this in two ways: First, he identifies a particular kind of sentence or grammatical construction that will help his students think and write in ways that are likely to come up in this particular writing unit or lesson, and then he introduces this idea in a mini-lesson at the beginning of the instruction. Then he focuses on other aspects of writing: making a plan, setting a goal, generating and organizing ideas, drafting and revising. Once students have a fairly solid draft of their writing that they are happy with, he returns to the grammar instruction that he started with and asks students to reread their own work with this element of writing in mind. He asks students to highlight an example of that usage or construction, or see if they might revise their sentences in a way to "give it a go" or try it out.

For example, when teaching argument writing, Tyler does a lesson on complex sentences, explaining to students that these are sentences that contain one independent clause and at least one dependent clause. He emphasizes how these sentences help provide more information about the main point, showing the relationship between ideas more effectively than a series of simple sentences.

Tyler tells students that when they write their claims, they might need to use a complex sentence to show relationships between ideas, like causes and effects, or to indicate that some lesser ideas are subordinate to ones they value more. He shows examples of these sentences, how they work, and how they are punctuated; he then gives students chances to find examples in the texts they are reading and share them with the class, highlighting independent and dependent clauses and encouraging but not overemphasizing that grammatical language. Soon he has them practice writing and punctuating some complex sentences outside of their main project for practice (but not too many). He may provide sentence stems as a scaffold for students if they are still working to own the concept. And then students get on with their main argument-writing practice.

When students begin the revision and editing processes, Tyler may make part of the peer-review process a close look at the claim in this piece of writing, using the language of complex sentences as they do so. He may ask a peer reviewer to "say back" to the writer what they expect the main idea of the paper to be and what other ideas will support it, and perhaps what conflicting ideas they expect the paper to address.

In a final edit and/or in a writer's memo reflecting on the process, Tyler may ask students to talk about how they crafted their thesis statement, whether they had to revise it and why, and whether sentence complexity helped them do something they did not know how to do before.

Tyler knows that ownership of usage and grammar support a developing writer, but he also knows that these are not the basis of good writing, that they are tools in a writer's toolbox more than rules to be followed, and that when he teaches grammar and usage in this way, students take it up and remember it.

Read More!

Bereiter, C., & Scardamalia, M. (1987). *The psychology of written composition*. Lawrence Erlbaum Associates, Inc.

Distinguishes between "knowledge-telling" and "knowledge-transforming" models of writing, explaining how expert writers actively reorganize and refine their ideas to construct meaning rather than merely recording information.

Braddock, R., Lloyd-Jones, R., & Schoer, L. (1963). *Research in written composition*. National Council of Teachers of English.

Reviews decades of studies on writing instruction and concludes that formal grammar instruction has no significant effect on improving students' writing ability.

Feldgus, E., & Cardonick, I. (1999). *Kid writing: A systematic approach to phonics, journals, and writing workshop*. McGraw-Hill.

Focusing on the youngest writers, demonstrates how activities that teach the print code as well as phonics can be integrated with methods that support composing, meaning-making, and communication.

Myhill, D. A., Jones, S. M., Lines, H., & Watson, A. (2011). Re-thinking grammar: The impact of embedded grammar teaching on students' writing and students' metalinguistic understanding. *Research Papers in Education, 27*(2), 139–166. https://doi.org/10.1080/02671522.2011.637640

Finds that embedding grammar instruction within the context of meaningful writing tasks, rather than teaching it in isolation, significantly improves students' writing quality and strengthens their metalinguistic understanding.

Weaver, C. (1979). *Grammar for teachers: Perspectives and definitions.* National Council of Teachers of English.

Divided into two sections, this book provides a theoretical explanation of the philosophy of grammar instruction and how to teach it productively, followed by a practical handbook-type section.

Myth 2: Writing Is a Set of Rules to Follow

One legacy of earlier emphases on classical rhetoric is the notion that there are a small number of set forms, each with their own rules, that writers must learn to reproduce. Reproducing the form correctly is thought to represent "good writing." But in reality, what is good writing depends on context, audience, and purpose. Writers make choices within and about types of writing in order to achieve their purposes. They may create an extended introduction for readers who need more background knowledge, or start with a short narrative to spark engagement before going into an argument. The rules many adult writers learned as children are made to be broken in the context of real writing.

The emphasis on rules includes the deeply held belief, at least in the United States, that there is one "correct" language for writing: Standard Written English (SWE) as an elite, academic language. The belief that English is the only acceptable language, like the belief that essays must have five paragraphs or that a thesis can only be at the beginning, can lead teachers to position writing as a set of fixed rules to be learned and followed, rather than an adaptive, meaning-making process. Additionally, privileging one form of language erases the linguistic diversity students bring to the classroom. It also takes away the possibility of learning from students' experience with multiple discourse communities, whether they be the resources of their home languages, social and professional groups, or even the language developing on the internet, sometimes referred to as "digitalk" (Turner et al., 2014).

When teachers treat writing as a set of rules to be followed rather than a strategic communicative process, students often focus on avoiding errors rather than developing their thinking or taking risks in their rhetorical decisions and linguistic choices. Research demonstrates that writing development is supported through inquiry-based and strategy-focused instruction that helps students apply discrete knowledge to specific contexts. Studies of discourse communities show that conventions are context-dependent and learned through participation in authentic practice.

Whereas overemphasis on formal correctness can limit a writer's rhetorical flexibility and growth, teaching students to analyze and engage with language and conventions that emerge from real social practices helps them to examine how genres and conventions vary across contexts. They can also come to understand that the "rules" are better understood as common choices writers may make to accomplish common purposes.

Research demonstrates that writing development is supported through inquiry-based and strategy-focused instruction that helps students apply discrete knowledge to specific contexts. By viewing the language communities students participate in outside of school, including home languages and dialects, as assets for learning, students can recognize that writing is socially situated, and identity is developed through language. This approach, also known as translanguaging, lets writers draw on the natural and dynamic use of their full linguistic repertoire to communicate and learn.

Practices to Destabilize	*Practices to Elevate*
• Presenting Standard Written English as the only "correct" language or dialect • Focusing grading on practicing text formulas rather than making choices to achieve a result	• Inquiry-based activities • Strategy instruction • Translanguaging and learning about language choices

Myth-Busting NWP Teachers At Work

Because Kara views her kindergarten students' home languages and dialects as assets rather than errors, she builds a writing environment where children learn that every language and every mode of communication is valued and allowed.

Her classroom is organized into writing stations, each with materials designed to spark ideas—objects, music, or thematic items tied to seasonal events. Children carry their journals from station to station, choosing where they want to work. They write in the ways that they know—through letters, words, symbols—all of which are acceptable.

Kara knows that they are making meaning even if they do not have the standard written language to express their thinking. When students do not know how to write a word, they might draw it, or perhaps include a phrase from their home language without translation.

Kara treats oral storytelling as writing, inviting students to "read" their pieces to her so she can hear the meaning behind their marks. Conferences unfold as warm conversations where she asks, "Who taught you that word? Would your classmates understand it? How might you help them learn it?"

The room features multilingual labels and vocabulary displayed in English, Spanish, and any other home languages represented. Students learn from one another, teaching classmates words from their families and seeing their linguistic identities honored.

Through this approach, Kara cultivates a space where translanguaging is normal, creativity comes first, and writing is an act of communication rather than correctness.

Read More!

Baker-Bell, A. (2020). *Linguistic justice: Black language, literacy, identity, and pedagogy*. Routledge.

Argues that schools should stop treating Black Language as "wrong" and instead affirm it as a legitimate, identity-rich language practice—changing literacy teaching and institutional policies to dismantle anti-Black linguistic racism.

Campbell, K., & Latimer, K. (2012). *Beyond the five paragraph essay*. Routledge.

Reviews research on the effectiveness of the five-paragraph essay form and provides strategies for teaching more creative, thoughtful, and purposeful writing instead.

Gort, M., Zapata, A., Seltzer, K., & Gómez, M., Eds. (2025). *Translanguaging perspectives on writing development and pedagogy: Learning from findings across teaching and learning contexts*. Emerald Publishing.

Recent research providing translanguaging perspectives on writing development and writing pedagogies across a variety of contexts. Chapters explore how a translanguaging lens can shift and expand notions of writing practices and instruction.

Graham, S., & Perin, D. (2007). A meta-analysis of writing instruction for adolescent students. *Journal of Educational Psychology, 99*(3), 445–476. https://doi.org/10.1037/0022-0663.99.3.445

Comprehensive meta-analysis that synthesizes decades of research on writing instruction, articulating evidence-based practices that most effectively improve writing, including engaging students in inquiry and generative activities

Hillocks, G. Jr. (1986). *Research on written composition: New directions for teaching*. National Conference on Research in English and ERIC Clearinghouse on Reading and Communication Skills. Eric # ED265552.

Comprehensive meta-analysis that synthesizes decades of research on writing instruction, demonstrating that inquiry-based, student-centered approaches are far more effective for improving writing than traditional grammar or skills-focused methods.

Smitherman, G. (1977). *Talkin and testifyin: The language of Black America*. Houghton-Mifflin.

Seminal text establishing the features and regularity of what has come to be called African-American Vernacular English. The text, and subsequent research, demonstrates that the AAVE is a complex and expressive English dialect of its own rather than an erroneous version of SWE.

Turner, K. H., Abrams, S. S., Katíc, E., & Donovan, M. J. (2014). Demystifying digitalk: The what and why of the language teens use in digital writing. *Journal of Literacy Research, 46*(2), 157–193. https://doi.org/10.1177/1086296X14534061

Examined linguistic features and rhetorical purposes of adolescent "digitalk," revealing it as a complex, adaptive form of communication that supports identity, audience awareness, and rhetorical flexibility.

Myth 3: Writing Is a Linear, Step-by-Step Process

Until the mid-20th century, writing instruction focused on a piece of writing as a finished thing—an essay, article, book, and so forth.

This perspective treated writing as a static outcome rather than a dynamic process of making and refining meaning. This view began to shift as research described the process of working writers, one that was an act of making meaning. Early research proved decisively that writers do not necessarily have a finished product in mind, but rather go through a process of discovering and refining what they think through the process of writing.

The early process movement of the late 20th century articulated the steps writers go through as they write, including prewriting activities like research, drafting, revising, and editing. This research was important in establishing a sense of the actual work writers engage in. Ironically, though, the neatly linear way in which the process was described as steps toward a finished product unintentionally reinforced a myth that continues to persist: that writing is a simple series of linear steps that always culminates in a specific product. The notion of a single writing process with a fixed number of steps took hold as a convenient heuristic to teach students about "the process."

Evolving from the early process movement, cognitive views of writing helped to reshape that conception of what the writing process is. Decades of research now show that writing is recursive, developmental, and socially mediated—not linear or solely product-oriented—and that writers move fluidly among planning, drafting, translating, and reviewing processes. The focus on what happens inside a writer's mind turned toward the influence of the rhetorical situation—or the intertwined nature of writers, audience, purpose, and contexts.

By the turn of the 21st century, the understanding that writing itself is an act of thinking, shaped by a social and cultural context, had evolved. Research helped to clarify that the act of composing helps writers discover and refine what they know. From this perspective, writing to understand what is known or believed is just as important—perhaps more important—as developing a polished product. Students benefit from having many opportunities to learn and explore ideas through writing without taking every piece through a full revision process culminating in a product to be assessed.

The view that the writing process is about producing products likely reinforces a linear process model of prewriting, drafting, revising, editing, and publishing. Teachers may worry that skipping any stage of the process will result in a weaker product. As a result, writing instruction can become formulaic and lockstep, with students moving through activities but not necessarily learning to navigate the recursive, messy nature of writing. Teachers who worry that a messy process will make assessment and grading challenging can emphasize the role of student reflection across individual pieces of writing by use of a writing portfolio or reflective memo that focuses on the writer's growth rather than the individual products.

Without messiness, students who move through a simple process will produce a piece of writing, but they will not likely learn to manage more complex topics or to deal with the roadblocks and confusions that inevitably arise in authentic writing contexts. Effective practice will help students understand that messiness, false starts, and turnarounds are all part of the experience of writing that even the most accomplished writers experience, but that effective writers have strategies for identifying the problems and solving them.

Practices to Destabilize	Practices to Elevate
• Taking every piece of writing through a complete process • Expecting every writer to work through writing on the same time frame and in the same way • Reading and grading everything written • Providing feedback only at the end	• Teaching process as problem-solving • Encouraging writing to learn without pressure of judgment • Providing feedback and collaboration at multiple stages • Teaching revision as meaning-making • Having students set goals and reflect on strengths and areas for improvement

Myth-Busting NWP Teachers at Work

Because they know students benefit from having many opportunities to learn and explore ideas through writing without taking every piece through a full revision process culminating in a product to be assessed, Sam's writing classroom is set up to ensure lots of time for noodling, tinkering, and practice, along with writing for assessment, publication, and other "endpoints."

In Sam's 4th-grade classroom, part of the back-to-school ritual is setting up writer's notebooks for every student. Students decorate their notebooks, and in other ways make them their own. These notebooks form a sort of home base for writing. Students keep lists of potential topics, do free-writing, and collect the writing that they do for "writing into the day" topics. Sam builds cycles of instruction throughout the year, knowing that each student writer will keep all of their exercises and first-draft writing in their writer's notebook. Besides teaching 4th grade, Sam is also an athletic coach, and as a writing teacher they "think like a coach." On the field Sam helps students create the habits of mind and practices to excel at their sport, and in class they create a culture in which students see how powerful, engaging, and, indeed, fun writing can be.

For instance, during the unit teaching argument writing, Sam helps their students see arguments not only based in study of literature or history, but the arguments that surround them in their lives. Because students may not have written arguments in school when they reach 4th grade, Sam creates a layer of instruction called routine argument writing to provide daily low-stakes practice opportunities for students to help them understand the genre of argument writing.

Routine argument writing happens at the beginning of class, and serves as a "bell ringer," the 5 minutes of warm-up writing that their administration requires at the beginning of a class period while a teacher takes attendance or checks in with individual students. However, Sam knows that if daily argument writing leverages the writing students are already doing; capitalizes on the habits of readers and writers; connects to the big picture of writers' lives, situations, and identities; is recursive, building on skills and returning to work already being done; and/or is generative, acting as seeds for work to come, then those few minutes each day are much more connected and productive than if they are each a stand-alone experience.

These short, sequenced writing into the day activities are designed to build toward an argument that Sam's students will write. These kinds of warm-up activities make efficient use of classroom time because they build fluency for Sam's students and, because they are carefully sequenced, give them experience with ever more complex tasks.

Also, these low-stakes writing experiences provide opportunities for Sam to see what students are already taking up without scaffolding. Moreover, during and after the drafting phase, Sam can note trends and patterns of argument moves, capture their noticings in a teacher notebook, and adapt their instruction to strengthen their students' argument writing.

Read More!

Emig, J. (1971). *The composing process of twelfth graders.* National Council of Teachers of English.

Examines the composing processes of adolescents, finding that writing is exploratory, not just product-based, and articulates a need for a change in the teaching of composition.

Flower, L., & Hayes, J. R. (1981). A cognitive process theory of writing. *College Composition and Communication, 32*(4), 365–387. https://doi.org/10.2307/356600

Finds that writing is a recursive process of planning, translating, and reviewing, not linear or product-centered.

Harris, K., Graham, S., & Mason, L. H. (2006). Improving the writing, knowledge, and motivation of struggling young writers: Effects of self-regulated strategy development with and without peer support. *American Educational Research Journal, 43*(2), 295–340.

Examines the effectiveness of self-regulated strategy development (SRSD), and finds that the model improved the writing skills, knowledge, and motivation of struggling young writers. The article demonstrates that SRSD instruction is more effective than a standard Writer's Workshop, leading to stronger performance in instructed and uninstructed writing genres and a deeper knowledge of writing. The addition of a peer support component further enhances the maintenance and generalization of these effects.

Hillocks, G. Jr. (1995). *Teaching writing as reflective practice.* Teachers College Press.

Argues that writing itself is a form of inquiry and that effective instruction engages students in investigating problems, testing ideas, and constructing meaning through the act of composing.

Muhammad, G. (2020). *Cultivating genius: An equity framework for culturally and historically responsive literacy.* Scholastic.

Demonstrates an equity-centered literacy model—rooted in Black literary traditions—that guides teachers to develop students' identity, skills, intellect, criticality, and joy through culturally and historically responsive instruction.

Whitney, A. (2021). *Growing writers: Principles for high school writers and their teachers.* National Council of Teachers of English.

Presents illustrations of research-supported practices at work in high school classrooms.

Yancey, K. B. (1998). *Reflection in the writing classroom.* All Utah State University Press Publications. https://digitalcommons.usu.edu/usupress_pubs/120

Develops a line of research based on the role of deliberative reflection in classroom contexts and offers a structure for discussing how reflection operates throughout a recursive writing process and across individual pieces of writing.

Myth 4: Writing Is Universal

The view that writing is about following a linear process to produce something that follows the rules of a specific form can lead to an expectation that the ability to write is easily transferable across contexts. For example, teachers and students alike may think that if they have mastered the five-paragraph essay and its rigid structure, they should be able to write a lab report. This approach assumes that mastering a single form ensures success in all writing contexts, and as a result, students often get repetitive practice within a limited range of genres.

Early work in genre theory, however, helped reframe genres not as static templates, but as tools through which people accomplish particular purposes. The lab report, for example, is structured as it is because of the demands of the scientific community. This line of research showed that genres evolve within disciplinary communities, carrying shared expectations that guide communication. Ultimately, the idea of discourse communities expanded into the understanding that literacy itself is more than just reading and writing. Rather, literacy is plural, and the concept of multiliteracies better reflects the diverse cultural, linguistic, and technological contexts in which people communicate.

Over the last few decades, research has documented that writing knowledge is domain-specific: Writers develop expertise through participation in communities of practice, and writing skills learned in one context do not automatically transfer to other settings without explicit support. In fact, writing is *situated,* meaning that what counts as "good" changes depending on the audience, genre, purpose, and community. A well-written lab report, for example, differs dramatically from a poem, an editorial, or a social media post. Movements such as writing across the curriculum and writing in the disciplines have developed curricula and practices to provide that support and help writers acquire the specific skills appropriate to the context in which they are working.

This insight, that writing is not a single, transferable skill but rather requires rhetorical awareness and flexibility, is an insight that can be taught. While writing teachers can't teach all the genres that writers will encounter, they can help writers learn to adapt to differences across contexts, apply prior learning in flexible ways, and negotiate discourse communities. Teaching writing as though there is only one formula can limit students' agility and creativity when they encounter new contexts. This is particularly important because digital tools are continually reshaping what writing is and therefore what makes it effective for particular audiences. In a world of evolving genres, media, and modes, writers must navigate and innovate within changing communication landscapes. By teaching students how to analyze and learn about "unfamiliar genres," we can equip them with the curiosity, openness, and skills needed to adapt to new requirements across their lives as writers.

Practices to Destabilize	Practices to Elevate
• Focusing on a limited range of types of writing • Teaching the essay as the only form of academic writing	• Writing in multiple forms, including emerging digital genres • Connecting writing across the curriculum • Learning how to learn about unfamiliar genres

Myth-Busting NWP Teachers at Work

Because Bryn knows that writing is situated, meaning that what counts as "good" changes depending on the audience, genre, purpose, and community, and that writers must learn to adapt to differences across contexts, apply prior learning in flexible ways, and negotiate discourse communities, she created the Rise Up & Write summer camp.

A youth advocacy writing camp for students in middle and high school, Rise Up & Write supports participants in understanding complex issues, imagining a better future, and using writing to create change by informing and engaging a variety of audiences. Adolescent writers in this camp are invited to explore an issue that they are interested in, invest time in inquiry and exploration of sources, and work through processes to help them gain a deeper understanding of the issue, such as understanding root causes and impact to individuals and communities.

Writers then create three resources on the same topic for slightly different audiences: peers, community, and change-makers. Depending upon their issue and what they are calling for, the medium for these three audiences might be different. For instance, a student might create an op-ed for their local paper, considering what readers of that paper might already know and think about their issue and what they hope to accomplish with their writing. They also could create a public service announcement focusing on a clear ask of listeners, and finally they might create a campaign button that puts their message into a pithy phrase and image that supporters of their cause would be excited to wear. By first inquiring and gaining a depth of knowledge and then thinking about multiple ways to use that knowledge, students in this summer writing experience gain flexibility and competence as decision-making (and change-making!) writers.

Read More!

Bazerman, C. (1988). *Shaping written knowledge: The genre and activity of the experimental article in science.* University of Wisconsin Press.

A classic text that explores how that genres are shaped by and within disciplinary communities.

Beaufort, A. (2007). *College writing and beyond: A new framework for university writing instruction.* Utah State University Press.

Shows that writing knowledge is domain-specific and transfer requires explicit instruction in rhetorical awareness

Early, J. (2022). *Next generation genres: Teaching writing for civic and academic engagement.* Norton Professional Books.

Introduces modern genres, from artist statements to podcasts, and unpacks how they work and how to make them.

Fleischer, C., & Andrew-Vaughn, S. (2009). *Writing outside your comfort zone: Helping students navigate unfamiliar genres.* Heinemann.

Demonstrates a wide range of inquiry-based activities that support students in investigating unfamiliar genres and learning about the conventions and priorities of writing in different discourse communities and disciplines.

Lent, R., & Voigt, M. (2018). *Disciplinary literacy in action: How to create and sustain a school-wide culture of deep reading, writing, and thinking.* Corwin.

Addresses content-area teachers directly, providing framework for keeping the subjects at the center while developing content-specific literacy.

New London Group. (1996). A pedagogy of multiliteracies: Designing social futures. *Harvard Educational Review, 66*(1), 60–92.

Introduces the concept of "multiliteracies," emphasizing that literacy practices are embedded in diverse social and cultural contexts.

Wardle, E. (2007). Understanding 'transfer' from FYC: Preliminary results of a longitudinal study. *WPA: Journal of the Council of Writing Program Administrators, 31*(1–2), 65–85.

Finds that writing learned in one context (e.g., composition class) rarely transfers automatically to other disciplines

Myth 5: Writing Is Best Done in Isolation

The image of a solitary writer, alone in a garret, struck by inspiration that produces a masterpiece in a single sitting, is a powerful cultural myth. By this point in the chapter, it should be clear that except on rare occasions, writing does not just spring forth from inspiration. It takes patient, hard work. Yet this is a myth that students as well as teachers still hold onto. Perhaps the most important thing that writing research has revealed is that writing is inherently *social.* Writers seek feedback from readers, engage in dialogue with others, write for audiences (real or imagined), collaborate, and participate in communities of practice. Writing is both a form of self-expression *and* an act of communication—a negotiation of meaning between writer and reader, shaped by purpose and context. The most effective writing classrooms emphasize this social element.

The belief that good writing emerges from individual genius, rather than social interaction, leads to instruction that emphasizes quiet, independent work, timed writing, and teacher-centered feedback in a way that is closer to an assessment context than the context of more authentic writing. When writing is viewed as a solitary act, teachers may feel that the only valid feedback comes from them—a heavy burden to carry. They may see any form of collaboration, including, perhaps, collaboration with AI, as compromising authenticity and originality. Yet research shows that the opposite is true: Practicing writers seek out and manage social connection as they work. Classrooms that provide for social interaction, peer response, and shared reflection are essential to the development of writers (Freedman, 1987).

Creating a community of writers who share writing and seek feedback helps students move from writing that centers their own thoughts, sometimes called "writer-based," to writing that anticipates and responds to the needs and expectations of others, called "reader-based" (Flower, 1979). Over time, students learn to navigate rhetorical situations with greater sophistication and empathy, understanding that writing always happens within a social context. They also learn more about themselves as they see how they come across to audiences.

Ultimately, treating the classroom as a community of writers creates opportunities for students to learn how to use peers and mentors, and how to seek out and provide help to others. When students leave the classroom, they do not go into the garret and wait for inspiration to hit; they need to have proactive strategies for moving through their writing process to accomplish their goals. They need to learn to listen to others, and also to listen to their "inner voice" and to sense what is working and not working in a piece of writing.

Of course, as part of a community, writers also learn another skill: namely, how and when to say, "Not now, I need some quiet time to write."

Practices to Destabilize	Practices to Elevate
• Emphasizing timed writing and assessment conditions for all writing • Disallowing conversation and collaboration in the writing classroom	• Writing for real audiences within and beyond classroom • Using writing groups, response partners, and Author's Chair to learn to give and receive feedback • Providing time for writing in the classroom • Teaching structured conversations about writing

Myth-Busting NWP Teachers at Work

Because Charlene and Shanterius know that writing is inherently social and that writers seek feedback from readers, engage in dialogue with others, write for audiences, collaborate, and participate in communities of practice, they have transformed a traditionally skills-focused college writing classroom into an active workshop community.

The classroom they share does not have the traditional rows seen elsewhere at the school; rather, they organize students around round tables where they can write during class time, move freely across the space, and collaborate with peers.

Neither Charlene nor Shanterius stands at the front of the room like many of their colleagues; instead, they circulate constantly, leaning in to confer with individual students or small groups. Sometimes they ask students to read their sentences aloud and prompt them to consider their audience and their rhetorical choices.

Students share drafts, not to correct each other, but to play with language. They experiment with tone, test profanity for rhetorical effect, weave in home languages, and adjust form. Whenever possible, authentic purposes ground their writing. For example, students initiated a writing campaign to university administrators regarding the campus food service.

What distinguishes these classrooms is that students are not simply compliant; they are engaging in collective problem-solving. They revise because ideas matter, because audiences are real, and because writing is a social and intellectual practice.

Read More!

Fecho, B. (2011). *Writing in the dialogical classroom: Students and teachers responding to the texts of their lives.* National Council of Teachers of English.

Provides illustrations of teachers building practice around the social and dialogical implications of viewing classrooms as communities of writers.

Flower, L. (1979). Writer-based prose: A cognitive basis for problems in writing. *College English, 41*(1), 19–37. https://doi.org/10.2307/376357

Introduces the concept of "writer-based prose" to describe early drafts that reflect the writer's internal thought structures rather than audience needs, proposing that effective writing instruction should help students transform writer-based into reader-based prose.

Gere, A. R. (1987). *Writing groups: History, theory, and implications.* Southern Illinois University Press.

Traces the historical development of writing groups and argues that they embody the inherently social nature of composing, positioning collaboration and peer response as central to writers' growth and learning.

Graham, S. (2018). A writer(s)-within-community model of writing. *Educational Psychologist, 53*(4), 258–279. https://doi.org/10.1080/00461520.2018.1481406

Proposes the writer(s)-within-community model to explain writing as a socially situated activity shaped by individual cognition, motivation, and self-regulation within the broader cultural, instructional, and community contexts that influence how writing develops.

Nystrand, M. (1986). *The structure of written communication: Studies in reciprocity between writers and readers.* Academic Press.

Explores the dynamic relationship between writers and readers, arguing that written communication is based on an understanding of expectations between writers and readers.

Spear, K. (1986). *Sharing writing: Peer response groups in English classes.* Boynton/Cook.

Demonstrates how peer response groups foster collaboration, audience awareness, and revision skills, showing that sharing writing in community helps students develop confidence and a deeper understanding of the writing process.

Vygotsky, L. (1978) *Mind in society: The development of higher psychological processes.* Harvard University Press.

Defines the Zone of Proximal Development (ZPD) as the distance between what a learner can do independently and what they can achieve with guidance from a more knowledgeable other.

AUTHORS' NOTE

Practicing writers, including the four who wrote this book, understand that even the best writers may struggle for ideas and sometimes follow paths that do not pan out. Even when the writing is polished and completely correct, it may not say what we want to say. Even when we strive for a specific form, we may find that it does not fit the need. As much as we might want a few solitary hours to work on a draft, we know we will benefit from hearing from others along the way and seeing how they approached a task. The truth is that sometimes scrapping a piece of writing and taking a different approach is the only way forward.

We struggled with this chapter. In fact, we struggled with the organization of this book for nearly 2 years as we worked through our composing process. We thought about our audience—and realized it was diverse. We wanted a book that spoke to all NWP teachers who had already read *Because Writing Matters* and *Because Digital Writing Matters,* providing them with the next step on a continuous journey of what the field has learned about teaching writing. We also wanted a novice teacher to open these pages and find a rich history in a digestible format that provides seminal and recent references without being too overwhelming *and* that provides a picture of classroom practice.

Ultimately, we decided that there are perpetual myths that continue to stand in the way of students, giving them the impression that challenges in writing are equivalent to a message that they *can't* write. As writers who teach writing, we want students to see that writing *is* a process where effective writers engage in the back-and-forth of problem-solving all along the way. And we believe the only way for students to gain this rich understanding of writing and the writing process is to be taught by myth-busting teachers.

CHAPTER 3

The Tools of Writing and Writers

In classroom spaces and personal screens, in handwritten journal entries, in formal essays submitted for a grade, in text messages and emails and sticky note reminders, in birthday cards and Instagram posts, writing is the lifeblood flowing through veins of everyday existence. Writing in all its forms not only still matters, it is a beautiful, essential part of the human condition.
—Rebecca Dimyan, Fairfield University

> Google Docs has all the polish of a typed paper, but allows me to see the student's eraser marks, without rips and pen smudges.
> —Sara Watkins Rock Ridge High School

Human-centered AI, grounded in best practices in pedagogy, will be as integrated as the typewriter, the computer, spell-checkers and other technologies that teachers have integrated over decades.
—Serena Morales, Boise State Writing Project

> Today's writer has so much magic at their fingertips when composing for others.
> —Bryan Ripley Crandall, Fairfield University

When the first NWP summer institute was held at UC Berkeley in 1974, typewriters with Wite-Out correction tape and library card catalogs with microfiche represented functional technologies for research and writing. But by the start of the 1980s, word processors had begun to change how writers worked. Even before computers became widely available, forward-thinking teachers began to teach the language of word processing in lessons on revision (e.g., copy, paste, move, delete) so that students would be ready to use personal computers when schools adopted them. However, mass adoption did not come quickly, and individual programs had different user interfaces, resulting in deep learning curves from one to the next. Even tech-savvy teachers wondered whether devoting classroom time to word processing was a good investment.

These kinds of questions were answered in the 1990s when software standardized the kinds of work done by the computer, and writers could transfer knowledge from one program to another, making instruction in revising and editing by word processor both doable and worthwhile. Shortly thereafter, "what you see is what you get" (WYSIWYG) editors afforded writers more control over design elements—font choice, clip art, headlines, and columns. This kind of design work, sometimes called desktop publishing, happened on a stand-alone machine, perhaps connected to a local network for printing, yet it dramatically expanded the potential products that teachers might invite students to create: flyers, banners, posters, and zines were examples of new modes that were afforded by new technologies. Desktop publishing represented a dramatic step forward from the simple copy/paste/move/delete of initial word processing.

Soon the ground shifted again, dramatically, with the advent of Web 2.0. Internet-connected computers could support publishing on "digital paper," first on blogs and then on social media. Although there were still plenty of printers for hard-copy versions of whatever was created, writers could produce content for delivery to a "screen," a much more malleable and connected destination than the products created with desktop publishing alone. Furthermore, students could learn to write in interconnected ways, placing hyperlinks within their writing that would take readers outside of the text they were creating to other texts, and they could include sound and motion, expanding possibilities for multimodal content beyond the use of image that desktop publishing afforded.

Throughout this journey from typewriter to Web 2.0, generations of teachers had to ask the same questions about any technology that entered the writing space: What is it? How does it work? What do we do with it as writers and in the writing classroom? Now, a quarter of the way into the 21st century, generative AI is inspiring conversations that sound remarkably similar to previous ones.

It would be a mistake to think that all this technology has reduced the importance of teaching writing by somehow making its production "easier." Quite the contrary. Thanks to the creation and spread of new technologies, humans of all ages are writing more than ever before and doing so in increasingly complex environments. Virtually every aspect of life is touched by internet-connected tools, apps, and digital environments. Writing takes place in mediated spaces where diversities of language, culture, and even worldview are the norm rather than the exception. Publication is instant, circulation is broad, and distant audiences can respond in seconds. Social media and group chats pressure writers to compose quickly and share without careful consideration of complex ideas, and the enduring digital footprint of the internet means that much of a writer's content will be traceable long into the future. The results of this ecosystem can be seen in public life and democratic institutions, and the introduction of artificial intelligence into the mix further complicates what it means to be a writer and to teach writing. In this complex time, writing matters more than ever, and conversations about what writing is and what writers do must account for the technologies that change the ways humans consume, create, connect, and communicate.

(RE)DEFINING DIGITAL WRITING

Literacy has always been intricately connected to technology, and each new advancement brings with it new ways of communicating—and often fear of the unknown. Socrates and Plato questioned the advent of writing itself, considering it an inferior form, with orality being the gold standard at the time (Ong, 2002). As Turner and Pankiewicz (2023) argued,

> The introduction of print through the printing press, screen-based writing through computers, networked writing through social media, and computer-generated writing through AI are all examples of moments when literacy practices changed, new norms needed to be developed, and humanity evolved. (p. 3)

In 2010, midway through the technology development described at the beginning of this chapter, NWP published *Because Digital Writing Matters* as a response to the rapid evolution of communication and information technologies that occurred in the decade after *Because Writing Matters. Because Digital Writing Matters* made the case for an intentional and sustained focus on technology in writing instruction in schools. The authors stated:

> Young people today have an unprecedented level of access to a wider range of content and connectivity than ever before, yet access does not ensure that reflection and learning take place. Student writers still need thoughtful and well-prepared teachers and mentors. Computers will not replace teachers, nor should they. Teachers of writing have a crucial role in supporting students in understanding the complexities of communicating in a twenty-first-century world. (p. 2)

Because Digital Writing Matters argued that unlike previous periods when schooling was a primary pathway to written literacy, contemporary students were more likely to engage with new digital technologies outside of school, and "school, in contrast, is seriously 'unplugged'" (p. 3). The book made the case that *digital* writing mattered and that teachers needed to understand "the dramatic changes in the ecology of writing and communication" (p. 4) that impacted the very nature of what it meant "to write—to create and compose and share" (p. 4). The game had changed, and the teaching of writing needed to change as well.

Since 2010, software has made most technical aspects of text creation easier, even on mobile devices, and young people are engaged in the real work of publishing and circulating their writing at ever younger ages. Although a 2008 Pew survey uncovered that teens did not think about the writing they did in digital spaces as "real" writing (Lenhart et al., 2008), now nearly all teens are composing on screens in school as well as in their personal lives. Digital *is* ubiquitous, and technologies have developed in ways that increase affordances for creation and publishing. For this reason, a revision is needed to the definition of digital writing adopted in *Because Digital Writing Matters*: "We define digital writing as compositions created with, and oftentimes for reading or viewing on, a computer or other device that is connected to the Internet" (p. 7). At the time, the internet itself provided opportunities not available to most writers who did not have access. Today, however, the landscape is different. Screen-based devices offer many apps that do not necessarily need internet connection, and technologies like Bluetooth enable sharing without being on the internet. Therefore, *any* writing done on a screen might now be considered digital writing, and it can be composed in a variety of forms—linear, nonlinear, networked—and modes, using a variety of media tools.

Over time the pace of technological change has increased, raising new questions for the next generation of teachers, learners, and writers. At this moment in time, artificial intelligence is transforming how content is created. "What writing is" is at another inflection point. Tools like ChatGPT, Gemini, Claude, and Copilot (to name a few) have the capability to generate text and images quickly, edit and revise existing compositions, and support research processes. The use of generative AI tools raises questions about ethical practices that are still being negotiated by communities of practice across disciplines and professions.

In *Teaching Writing in the Age of AI: Strategies for Teachers of Secondary Students,* Hicks and Turner (2025) argued that teaching writers to use AI as a support, rather than a crutch, is an important part of the work of teachers in an age of AI. They provided a framework of seeing AI as (a) a thinking partner, (b) a research assistant, and (c) a co-writer. It is the third category that truly redefines "what writing is," and it is an area where critical conversations are needed moving forward. If software can co-write, what is it that writers do?

Critical conversations are happening as teachers and students debate what it means to use AI in writing. For instance, what are the ethical boundaries between co-writing and cheating? Interestingly, Mah et al. (2024) uncovered tensions between student perspectives and teacher perspectives in defining cheating using AI. This generational divide could be indicative of socially normed practices that are different across life spans. It could also suggest areas where writing teachers—and writers themselves—need to redefine what it means to struggle through a writing process. Ubiquitous support can create dependencies, but writers can also develop their own processes that adopt a variety of tools to help them share their ideas and voice. Writer agency requires independence, autonomy, and authority to make these decisions. With a long-term developmental vision that teachers want writers to grow, they can consider, together, what is healthy and helpful, and what is not.

INTENTIONAL INTEGRATION OF TECHNOLOGY FOR AUTHENTIC PRACTICE

This transformational moment requires an even greater shift away from product-oriented writing, a shift that the National Writing Project has called for in previous publications. Writing instruction must put emphasis on developing the writer, not just on the product created. Helping writers grow as thoughtful, reflective, strategic creators who can effectively take advantage of the new affordances technology provides is ultimately more important than any individual piece. Developing ideas, understanding audiences, and working through feedback and revision is hard but important work. Teaching writers in this new era involves helping them to identify when a struggle is not productive versus when it is helpful to move their thinking and writing forward.

This stance—of putting writers at the center of a writing classroom—allows teachers to focus on developing literacies through authentic use of technology rather than incorporating technology into instruction for the sake of technology alone. This kind of pedagogy focuses on intentional integration of the tools of writers and writing, and it requires rethinking assessment with primary attention to process, rather than product. Admittedly, the structures of school, including policies and societal norms that place value on tested forms of writing, sometimes make it challenging to reframe practice; however, writing project teachers have been pushing boundaries for a long time, and examples of effective pedagogy continue to be developed and shared.

At the time of publication of *Because Digital Writing Matters*, writers had shifted from word-processing platforms to an internet-based experience where collaboration across time and space was possible. Vignettes of classroom practice from that book highlighted both the possibilities of using video and audio in writing, as well as the ability for students to write together on a single document and respond to each other's work. The following example showcased rich possibilities from that time:

> A pair of high school teachers—one English teacher and one social studies teacher—plan a multiweek unit in which their students will engage in community-based research and represent their work as a digital story or short film at a final exhibition night. Students begin by generating topics and questions that they would like to ask members of

> their community and posting those ideas to a project wiki, one shared by multiple sections of these two teachers' classes throughout the day. Over the course of the project, students collect artifacts with digital tools such as voice recorders and video cameras, documenting their work on the project wiki. Once the videos are produced, a process that takes nearly two weeks of gathering, organizing, editing, and merging media, students celebrate by inviting the community members they interviewed to the school for the exhibition night. Eventually, many videos are posted on a video-sharing site to allow people from outside the community to see what the students have discovered in their research.

Fifteen years later, opportunities for writing have expanded as teachers harness the positive benefits of information and communication technologies. For example, in Drew Writing Project Teacher Consultant Jill Stedronsky's 8th-grade classroom in 2025, students pursued yearlong inquiries, consuming a variety of texts (traditional, video, audio, image-based) as they developed, revised, and sometimes redirected their questions. They connected with students from other countries, wrote essays for real audiences (e.g., *The New York Times*), and created in multiple modes as they honed their thinking and their arguments. At the end of the year, they created TED Talks that brought together the results of their inquiries and submitted them to TED-Ed for potential publication. Throughout their reading and writing processes, they engaged with generative AI as thinking partner, research assistant, and co-writer (Hicks & Turner, 2025) to push their thinking and their writing forward.

Jill's classroom reflected an authentic use of technology rather than a "technology integration" mindset—that is, integrating technology as technology rather than as the practices of writers. In this space writers engaged in authentic practices in school so that they became critical consumers and creators outside of school in the spaces where they existed daily. Writing teachers who intentionally integrate the development of digital literacies (Hicks & Turner, 2026) into writing instruction support this kind of authentic work.

NEW PRIORITIES FOR AN AGE OF UBIQUITY AND ABUNDANCE

The kind of class setting and practice Jill has created would not have been possible until her school adopted 1:1 device accessibility and consistent internet connectivity. The COVID-19 pandemic pushed schools forward in investing in technologies that would allow all students to consume and create digital texts, making digital devices ubiquitous and access to information abundant. Now, most children and adolescents have access to devices both in their homes and at school that allow them to consume and create constantly. They are "always on" (Baron, 2008). Young writers can be more ambitious, creative, and collaborative, but they also face higher stakes.

The profound shift to digital content that is always available on devices that teens (and adults) carry all the time has been challenging. Social media, which has only grown in importance since *Because Digital Writing Matters* was published, has impacted the information ecosystem in disruptive ways, and research has begun to document the damaging effects it can have on teens in particular. Information literacy has become a central concern in many classrooms, as misinformation and "AI slop" (Mahdawi, 2025) fill social media feeds run by algorithms that push information that has neither been vetted nor actively searched. Research has begun to document the impact on critical thinking and extended literacy on both youth and adults as humans spend more time with short-form content and less time with long-form text (Carr, 2010; Organisation for Economic Co-operation and Development [OECD], 2019; Wolf, 2018). All technology comes with both affordance and limitations, and the negative impacts of ubiquitous technology have social consequences that cannot be ignored, even as they are only just beginning to be understood.

This new landscape requires specific focus on curricular priorities that have been hovering in the background since the publication of *Because Digital Writing Matters*. In particular, the following areas are increasingly significant: multimodal composition, information literacy, and the ethics of participation. The impact on literacy practices that technology has brought requires shifting priorities. Areas that were just beginning to be realized in 2010 must now become central in writing classrooms, even as new technologies like generative AI bring additional anxieties to already overwhelmed educators. With intentionality, teachers can connect writing instruction in schools with the digital lives of students outside of school and develop skills of consuming, creating, connecting, and collaborating in critical and ethical ways.

Multimodal Composition

In the years surrounding the publication of *Because Digital Writing Matters*, composition and linguistic researchers paid significant attention to "multimodality." New digital tools afforded writers opportunities to blend text, image, audio, video, and even movement in interesting ways and for powerful effects. A leader in this area, Kress (2010), argued, "There are domains beyond the reach of language, where it is insufficient, where semiotic-conceptual work has to be and is done by means of other modes" (p. 15). Although Palmeri (2012) made a case that multimodality had been referenced throughout the history of composition theory development, citing examples such as "Geneva Smitherman's powerful critique of the conventional privileging of print forms of knowledge in the academy" (p. 5) and "Donald Murray's fascination with the intersections between photography and writing," he accurately assessed that the general tone of research in the early 21st century suggested that "alphabetic literacy is our past; multimodal composing is our future" (p. 5).

Indeed, technological developments like the smartphone in 2007 made it possible for individuals to capture images and video that could be embedded into writing. Researchers like Cope and Kalantzis (2009), Mills (2010), and Jewitt (2008) pushed conversations about the changing nature of literacy into the need for schools to respond to the moment, which centered on a "digital turn" (Mills, 2010) that invited multimodal creation.

Although *Because Digital Writing Matters* highlighted teachers whose practices emphasized multimodal practices, at the time the book was drafted, the concept of multimodality was not fully embedded in the digital practices of youth. In the years since, however, new technologies and easily accessible applications, along with the ubiquity of smartphone ownership, have made it possible for everyone to combine text, image, sound, and video as part of a meaning-making process. Indeed, as social media platforms became dominant community spaces on the internet, the short video and the audio podcast took hold as major forms of composition. In these modes, text was represented in different ways, with alphabetic text sometimes being completely hidden from a reader's (or consumer's) view. Some platforms that became popular, especially with young people (e.g., TikTok), were inherently multimodal, offering tools within the app to streamline the composing process. Thus, while

Palmeri (2012) was correct that multimodality had always been connected to compositionists' thinking, in contemporary times, multimodal creation is part of daily life for many writers.

Perhaps ironically, many people do not see their creation of video, social media posts, or memes (to name a few) on a daily basis as "writing," and it is likely a prejudice that privileges traditional forms of alphabetic text-based composition that has limited large-scale adoption of curricula that center multimodal writing instruction. In fact, these daily acts represent the products of people's thinking, their desire to connect and/or share a message with others, and their understanding of purpose and audience. Every user of social media who adds content to the platform is a writer, and it is important for youth to recognize the responsibilities of being a writer in a public space.

To center multimodal writing as a curricular priority is to bring the outside world into the classroom. Building on the work of Hillocks (1995) and Smith et al. (2012), Hicks et al. (2013) articulated the knowledge that digital writers need, including knowledge of content, form, and technology. In multimodal writing, they argued, knowledge of technology deepens the ways in which writers are able to apply knowledge of content and form. As multimodal writers develop, they need opportunities to play with a variety of technologies so that they can learn what tools afford—and how they might constrain—them as they consider their language, audiences, and purposes in writing.

Many teachers have experimented with multimodal writing and embraced the need to incorporate it intentionally into instruction. For example, Andy Schoenborn of the Chippewa River Writing Project has his high school students conduct self-inquiry to define the values they hold and turn this inquiry into a multimodal blog post. As a component of this writing, they generate images using AI in order to create personal avatars that showcase the values they uncovered. This kind of practice allows students to play with technologies, to consider how modes work together to make meaning, and to develop skills of creation in the forms that represent real-world writing.

Information Literacy

An early study of Twitter found that the social media network, less than 3 years old at the time, supported "a fast diffusion of information" (Kwak et al., 2010). Platforms like Twitter allowed users to share information quickly to a global audience, but because of the instantaneous nature of sharing, vetting of information was virtually nonexistent for over a decade, and mis- and disinformation spread easily. Now social media platforms sometimes choose to suppress or promote particular kinds of information, and algorithms cater to anger and fear—emotional responses that make it difficult for users to discern facts or to engage productively in conversations.

Wardle (2020) suggested that "we live in an age of information disorder," and Wardle and Derakhshan (2017) outlined seven types of mis- or disinformation that impact the "information ecosystem," which is "dangerously polluted and dividing rather than connecting us" (Wardle, 2020, para. 1). Vosoughi et al. (2018) found that "falsehood diffused significantly farther, faster, deeper, and more broadly than the truth in all categories of information, and the effects were more pronounced for false political news than for false news about terrorism, natural disasters, science, urban legends, or financial information" (Abstract). Although in recent years some social media companies have started to track and identify potentially false or misleading information, depending on the company's ownership, the commitment to fact-checking is not consistent over time. Therefore, it is incumbent upon writers to evaluate, confirm, and potentially qualify information before sharing it with others.

But assessing information quality is challenging in fast-paced online environments that prioritize speed of response and incentivize emotion-producing content. Schools, then, play an essential role in actively promoting standards of research and evaluation of information and teaching strategies for information literacy in a digital age.

Digital and information literacy have come a long way since the early days, which emphasized finding webpages via search engines and assessing credibility with simple techniques. At the beginning of the 21st century, "fake" websites were fairly easy to identify. Today, however, it is easy to create sites, news content, and other information resources that look high-quality yet are not credible. It is also true that credibility exists along a continuum, with few websites being entirely fraudulent as opposed to a mixture of good and bad information. As a result, more sophisticated strategies, such as Mike Caulfield's SIFT or lateral reading strategies popularized by Sam Wineberg, both promoted in their book *Verified* (Caulfield & Wineberg, 2023), have been adopted. Additionally, organizations such as News Literacy and Common Sense Media specialize in resources and curricular content with an emphasis on navigating the current information environment.

Given that half of adult information consumers now name social media sites as a primary source of news and information (Pew Research Center, 2025), it is important that students acquire a basic understanding of how these platforms work, including the role of algorithms and the way that interactions with a platform shape the content they receive. Given the shaping power of platforms and algorithms, students need to understand how and when to jump outside of social media to search for information from credible sources and experts.

The ability to gather and use information in writing has always been important; in contemporary times, writers need to develop strategies that help them navigate an abundance of information in order to ensure that they are considering multiple perspectives, sourcing quality evidence, and sharing accurate information. Writing teachers can no longer rely on instruction in evaluating credible websites; more nuanced examinations of author, purpose, presentation, and funding/incentives are necessary. Similarly, writers must develop ethical stances that support their participation in society and the digital ecosystem in which they exist.

Ethics in a Participatory Culture

For many years, teaching ethics in the writing classroom was closely aligned with ethical practices in academic writing: Avoid plagiarism, cite correctly, and don't copy word for word. Although these lessons were important, many times classroom discussions seemed to focus more on rules and formulas than the principles that are more properly called "ethics."

Technology, however, has broadened and deepened the need for discussions about ethics. Now that many young writers are authentically participating and publishing on digital platforms, their ethical decisions have real consequences, positive or negative, in the world. For example, students who eagerly circulate misinformation on social media platforms or, perhaps, stretch the truth themselves actively contribute to polluting the information ecosystem. Students who take the time to check sources, write community notes, or identify and report problems help clean the same ecosystem.

The old standbys of citation and credit still apply, though students are as likely to hyperlink as to footnote, but they may now include practices for the use of digital assets, understanding of fair use and Creative Commons, and questions about attribution of ideas generated in online spaces or modeled after other students. When students record people and places, there are questions of privacy and protection of the identity of others. Many of these latter concerns might come under the heading of good digital citizenship and already have a place in that curriculum.

Still, it is important for writing teachers to incorporate specific lessons on ethical practice in the context of digital, multimodal writing. When can students use images they have not created? Should they post a picture of a friend without permission? In what circumstances might they find themselves in an ethical struggle about whether to reshare content? Each of these questions ultimately comes back to audience, purpose, and impact of message—the core of writerly choices.

GenAI inspires new conversations about ethical practice that also cannot be ignored in the context of writing, writers, and writing instruction. On a continuum of "more AI work" and "more human work" (Miller, 2023), questions like, "What's okay? What's not? For whom? Under what circumstances?" can (and should) be topics of conversation in the writing classroom. As communities of practice develop—and push back on—new ethical norms, students can also grapple with these issues.

It is likely that novice writers will make ethical missteps. Even adults with fully formed brains sometimes struggle with ethical practice in writing. Ultimately, the writing classroom can be a safe space where students learn about, grapple with, and try on what it means to participate—so that they can develop the ethical standards needed to responsibly contribute their writing in the digital world.

Challenges Ahead

The digital ecosystem that has developed in the last 3 decades has created the ability for anyone to publish anything, anywhere, instantaneously, and without the gatekeepers that had come to define previous eras. In some ways, the internet has democratized and expanded writing; in other ways, technology has limited digital content through platforms that enforce particular design choices and manage content through algorithms created by humans and implemented by machines.

Writing teachers now face the excitement and the challenge of knowing that every student in their classroom can take their writing—authentically—from inception through development and design, to publication, circulation, and beyond. Humans are all writers who can share ideas broadly in diverse modes. Yet, while it may seem like technological innovations have created opportunities for all individuals to have a voice in society, the benefits of access come with complications.

All communities can now have digital access to share and publish without large-scale financial investment needs to communicate ideas, which has historically been a barrier to publishing diverse perspectives. Students need opportunities. Opportunities for apprenticeship, mentoring, and editorial review for young writers must be cultivated carefully to provide writers with real pathways to learning. Developing writers still need models and mentors, and teachers need to draw attention to the ethics of participation in digital spaces. Helping novice writers to navigate information by slowing down, reading intentionally, and creating moments of friction in their writing and publishing process is much more critical than it used to be. In the emerging age of generative AI, teachers can serve as lead learners in the writing classroom by asking questions about the costs, benefits, and social impact of any tool in the composing process.

AUTHORS' NOTE

In the years since the publication of *Because Digital Writing Matters,* there has been an explosion in the nature, number, and kinds of tools for writing. And as teachers, we are often filled with questions that can sometimes be overwhelming. We are now grappling with the impact of GenAI on writing, something our author team did throughout the process of writing this book. With Kristen advocating to push *through* the technology and claim our writerly agency, Elyse raising societal impacts, and Tanya pushing back, arguing for critical views of GenAI, our team had lively meetings. We posited, we challenged one another, we evolved as writers and as a writing team. By the time Tonya brought an AI-generated profile of a writing classroom of the future to one of our conversations, we had coalesced around the words written in this chapter and embraced GenAI—if not individually, at least as a collective—as a tool to push our thinking.

We know there are big questions that still need to be explored, but what we have learned over time is that the answer, as always, is not in the tools but in the writers. As Garcia (2019) has said, "There is no algorithm or platform that can replace the meaningful interactions that can stem between teachers and students" (p. xiv). The tools of writers and writing will continue to evolve; the heart of writing does not change.

CHAPTER 4

Writing Reaches Beyond

> Our stories, told in our own words, in all the ways that we as people like to tell our stories, are important. The history of our experiences is the foundation for our civilization and all that will remain of us after we are gone.
>
> —Ana Contreras, Harper College

As an educator, I write to engage with students because I want to be aware of what they are feeling, thinking and planning to do. I write to my peers and friends because I want to hear their accomplishments, I want to be inspired by their creative energy and passion. I write to older generations because I need to be aware of their concerns about the future and trajectory of our world.
—William Joseph King, Central High School

> To have an idea in the metauniverse of ideas, and then to express it in a way that connects humanity to a greater ongoing conversation, is the means by which we move forward. The act of pen to paper, that intentional choice to organize thoughts and keep memories, means that we can ponder the moments of our collective cares, and build empathy for all of our voices and stories. The choice of that action, to consciously write down eternalness of our hearts' passions and fears, means that we are connected to the human condition across space and time.
> —Gretchen Monroe, Lincoln Christian School

In the decades since the publication of *Because Writing Matters,* two significant trends have shaped the teaching of writing: accountability and assessment inside schools, and the digital revolution outside of school. For most of this period, the public discussion of writing has focused on the results of standardized tests, resulting in panicked press proclaiming that students could not write. As a result, policymakers increased testing and amped up accountability measures for schools. According to Hillocks (2002), the result was a narrowing of writing pedagogy to the testable forms, modes, prompts, and audiences of standardized tests—a result that many National Writing Project teachers also documented as they saw the impact of annual testing on student skills and motivation, even as they pursued strategies for students to engage in real work by "writing for a change" (NWP et al., 2006).

Yet during this period of high-stakes testing, families and schools also began to seriously invest in digital tools and platforms, expanding device and internet access both in school and at home. With new digital tools for writing, media-making, and social connection, young people explored opportunities to write for real audiences and purposes outside of school, and the contrast with formulaic writing inside of schools was palpable. NWP teachers were eager to learn what their "creative and connected" students were doing that could point the way to more engaged and authentic writing experiences in their classrooms. Teachers could see the possibilities for teaching writing that reached beyond—beyond the classroom walls, beyond teacher and peers as audience, and beyond the limitations of school-based genres—to reach real audiences and serve real purposes in the civic and community sphere.

REAL VS. ROTE WORK

As we described in Chapter 2, writing researchers have long been influenced by the processes of practicing writers. Texts like *A Writer Teaches Writing* by Donald Murray (1968), a Pulitzer Prize–winning journalist, have become common readings in professional development circles at both the K–12 and the higher education levels, and scientific research on "what writers do" has influenced developing best practices in pedagogy. Across reflections and studies of writers at work, theorists could see a wide array of activity that was part of "writing": observational note-taking, playful sketching, list-making and annotating, as well as more conventional drafting and redrafting. Some of the work of writing was clearly for the benefit of the writer alone—a way of thinking through a puzzling idea or testing out approaches to something.

But regardless of the diversity of the activities of writing, from quickly scribbled thoughts to lengthy revision and editing tasks, practicing writers understood that they were purposefully pointing in the direction of real work and, generally, toward real audiences and purposes. At its heart, writing eventually goes public, and public writing is an attempt to do something (move people, change their minds, make them laugh, etc.) to someone (an intended audience).

The NWP has always been interested in finding ways for students to write for real audiences and purposes, even within the confines of school. Teachers implemented "authentic writing" practices, in contrast to the test-based or worksheet-driven activities that Hillocks (2002) lamented. To learn to write well, writers need a chance to see what it is like to write for real audiences and purposes so they can come to understand the strategic nature of the decisions writers make. The outcome of a successful, or even unsuccessful, attempt at real writing is more than a score on a standardized test or a grade in a gradebook. It is the result of the effort, of the productive struggle, of the work of writing.

More recently, the vocabulary of "authenticity" is used less—after all, isn't all writing in some way authentic? However, the notion that writing becomes *real* when it matters to the writer either personally or professionally is still important. In his book *The Real Work: On the Mystery of Mastery,* Gopnik (2023) described the difference between accomplishment and achievement as he reflected on the idea of "real work":

> We all know the real work in whatever field it is we've mastered. It's shorthand, one might say, for the difference between accomplishment and mere achievement, the assigned work. Yet the real work doesn't seem to be a goal of the way we live, which favors, over the real work, what we might call the rote work. We live in an achievement-driven society in which kids of all kinds are perpetually being pushed toward the next evanescent achievement instead of the next enduring accomplishment. (p. 2)

This distinction between the next evanescent achievement (made often by rote work) and the next enduring accomplishment (the hallmark of real work) is a similar reflection on the difference between the kinds of writing traditionally taught in schools, especially in response to a culture that values test scores, and the kinds of writing that youth do outside of school. The hard work of learning to write must be *for something,* and for that something to be powerful, it cannot be an opportunity to do something great in a far-off future that a young person can barely imagine; it has to be something great that they can do right now—something that matters to the individual writer. Whether it is moving an audience to laughter or tears, or convincing fellow citizens to believe or do something, teachers can help writers reach audiences and experience the accomplishment of doing something *real* with their writing. Or, perhaps even more importantly, they can help students see how writing is an important part of the work they may already be doing outside the classroom in their digital and civic lives.

AUTHENTIC YOUTH PRACTICES

Young people have always written beyond the boundaries of school, but digital life has fundamentally expanded what "authentic writing" looks like. In the age of the read-write web—and now an AI-enhanced participatory internet—it is easy for individuals to share their ideas and voice far beyond their classroom and even their community. For many, this reach feels empowering; for others, it has led to moments of misunderstanding, conflict, or unanticipated consequences. These realities make it essential for educators to understand *how* youth participate in digital spaces, as well as the cultural and social ecosystems that shape their practices. Authentic youth writing cannot be separated from the networked spaces where they create, collaborate, circulate ideas, and, often, take risks that they would not take in school settings. Students need to learn to be both brave and safe and to participate ethically in public spaces, recognizing that there are both intended and unintended audiences.

The research of the Connected Learning Alliance (CLA) has shaped understanding of how to support young writers in their real writing outside of school by considering what it means to be a connected learner. The CLA, originally funded by the MacArthur Foundation and currently stewarded by the Connected Learning

Lab at the University of California, Irvine, brought together educators, librarians, researchers, game designers, technologists, and media producers to explore how learning can be anchored in authentic youth practices while still being academically robust and socially meaningful. As a result of years of research, the Connected Learning framework articulates that "Learning is irresistible and life-changing when it connects personal interests to meaningful relationships and real-world opportunity" (Connected Learning Alliance, n.d.). Connected Learning represents "real work," where youth can accomplish in areas where they are passionate and supported.

As a founding member of the CLA, NWP helped teachers lean into learning about youth's self-sponsored literacy practices in the digital age, particularly their practices outside of school. What NWP teachers noticed was that youth were deeply engaged in interest-driven, peer-connected creative production. They wrote fan fiction, created commentary on a variety of social platforms, composed poetry, participated in gaming worlds, and advocated for causes that mattered to them. Their literacies in these spaces were shaped by identity, community, and participation.

Educators who researched these authentic practices and spaces realized that the creativity and engagement students displayed outside of school often exceeded what they did in the classroom. The conditions were markedly different, likely because of the difference in the foundational purpose of real versus rote writing tasks. Additionally, the CLA line of research made it clear that young people need adult mentors to navigate the ethical, civic, and emotional complexities of writing in public spaces. When writers participate online, they encounter real audiences and real consequences. They need to see their agency as writers in these spaces and participate responsibly.

Understanding authentic youth practices over the last decade (or more) through the Connected Learning framework has made it clear that writing instruction must extend beyond the classroom walls. Teaching writing means acknowledging the digital spaces where young people participate and helping them to see the work that they do outside of school as *real* writing. It means designing opportunities where students can write for meaningful audiences, cultivate their voices, and develop a sense of responsibility. In this way, teachers can help young writers be active participants in the world they are helping to shape.

Real Audiences

While educators might think of public writing as the purview of high school students, teachers of very young children can create opportunities for those students to engage with the world through writing. Such opportunities can provide real audiences for the youngest writers, creating a driving purpose to work hard as a writer. They also provide teachers with a way to reframe negative views of schools and their learners, and to argue for writing instruction that honors the experiences and choices of writers.

For example, in 2017, with support from an LRNG Innovators Challenge Grant, a team of six rural elementary teachers from Bastrop, Texas, led by Katie McKay, a Teacher Consultant with the Heart of Texas Writing Project, embarked on a yearlong journey of deep professional development to bring Connected Learning to their writing workshop classrooms. Calling their project *Choice and Voice: Agency and Audience in a Resilient Rural Texas Community,* they began their work by setting up student-driven classrooms and projects and creating a responsive curriculum to grow authentic, enthusiastic, and motivated writers in their rural Title I kindergarten, 2nd-, and 3rd-grade classrooms. In many ways, their work would have looked like standard, high-quality, collaborative curriculum revision. But the ambition to reach audiences beyond the confines of the classroom led them to plan writing workshop units of study that would begin with student choice of topic and culminate in publication in the local community and digitally: choice and voice.

For instance, Shirley Miller's kindergarten class published stories from their own lives through drawings and words. The student writing was made available via QR codes at a school publication party and then displayed in the community at Berdoll's Pecan Candy and Gift Co. Using a digital platform, visitors to Berdoll's were able to read the writing and follow the QR codes to hear the kindergarteners speak. Miller's students also applied author's craft in ABC books to their own original digital and print ABC books. Their classroom ABC books were shared on the local Bastrop Public Library server, and their individual hard-copy books were displayed at the Bastrop Library.

Mrs. Kim Russell's 2nd-grade class wrote fiction books and, with the support of the Bastrop children's librarian, displayed their books at the local Bastrop Public Library for readers to enjoy. Dr. Guadalupe Chávez's bilingual kindergartners wrote *libros informativos*, or informational books, about topics they knew about through personal experience and research. They shared their informational books at a classroom publication party with their parents and school staff as well as online.

In many places, students like these in Bastrop—students whose families experience financial hardships, students who are learning English as an additional language—find themselves in classrooms that focus in limiting ways on the basics: phonics, spelling, correctness. They are stuck in a spiral of rote work with limited—if any—opportunity to engage in real work. McKay and her team wanted more for their students, namely for them to be learning through the accomplishment of writing and sharing their own stories with their community.

Taking the student work public was a way to validate their practices and to demonstrate the students' capacity. Students' work was often displayed with explanations about the importance of meaningful literacy engagements, the utility of invented spelling to develop literacy skills, and the markers of growth that can be seen in imperfect work. But more importantly, creating stories and books for audiences beyond the classroom helped students to see themselves as writers, and helped the school district and community see what young writers could accomplish.

This kind of real work at the middle and high school level can also be lost to overemphasis on achievement in standardized testing. However, NWP teachers have made authentic audiences a reality.

Real Purposes

For many young people, writing is framed almost exclusively as preparation for the future: the essay that will get them into college, the placement exam they must pass, the "college-level writing" that will matter someday.

The stakes are, of course, undeniably real. Writing functions as a gatekeeper to postsecondary success, particularly for students from rural and underresourced schools, for students of color, and for multilingual learners. Nearly one-third of first-year students enroll in remedial courses before they can access credit-bearing classes. Such courses can ultimately keep young people, especially low-income students, from completing college. Research is unequivocal: Strong reading and writing skills are foundational to success across disciplines, yet college instructors consistently report that incoming students struggle to generate ideas, marshal evidence, and organize arguments (ACT, 2016).

However, telling young people that they need to work hard to prepare for a far-off future, one that they may not yet envision, is rarely motivating enough to help them engage in the sustained practice required to develop complex writing skills. Just as student athletes need real, immediate opportunities to put their skills to the test, young writers need real opportunities to share their burgeoning skills and get feedback from real audiences. They need writing to matter in the lives they are living today.

This is the grounding principle in the College, Career, and Community Writers Program (C3WP). The framework helps teachers ground their teaching of argument writing to scaffold the development of cognitive skills and strategies that students will need to succeed in college, and it does so by rooting instruction in issues that are local, immediate, and relevant to their lived experiences. C3WP classrooms engage real purposes: Students investigate issues that affect their communities, write to audiences beyond the teacher, and do the real work of argumentative writing as a tool for participation. Students in C3WP classrooms come to understand that they CAN write arguments, that their arguments can make a difference in the world, and that because arguments are powerful, they have to engage them with care and responsibility.

When students write for real purposes, the results can be powerful. In Alabama, 4th-grade students wrote letters to the principal suggesting ways to make their school better on topics as varied as school lunch, after-school sports, and new units for gym class. In Kentucky, one high school put together an argument-writing fair that was hosted in the mall. Students presented their work, which ranged from proposals for helping unhoused members of their communities to supports to end drug addiction to proposed assistance for the local animal shelter, via posters and discussion to local shoppers, creating not only interest in their topics, but support for the school and its writing program. In Columbus, Montana, students wrote an op-ed arguing for a local referendum that would raise taxes to pay for advanced life-saving services in their community. Their piece ran in their local newspaper and contributed to the referendum's passage.

Although not every piece of writing can—or should—lead to a policy change or political action, the opportunity to speak publicly and see that writing is a form of action brings real purposes to classroom practice. This kind of work not only improves students' writing skills, but also helps to cultivate a writerly identity in students. Students with skills *and* the opportunity to use them, not in some distant future but right now, see themselves as writers, writers who use writing to accomplish things in the world today.

Building Agency

Building agency in young writers means that they see themselves not just as vessels who receive knowledge and regurgitate it, but as contributors who create, question, and use knowledge to shape their worlds. In an era when information is abundant, this shift is essential. Today's learners need opportunities to make knowledge. The following examples illustrate what it can look like when students develop agency through out-of-school learning. Many of these projects are rooted in skills of historical thinking (asking questions, interpreting evidence, and revising claims), which offers a powerful context for a writing classroom. When young people practice this kind of cross-disciplinary thinking, they learn that their interpretations—and their voices—matter both in and out of the classroom.

As part of the NWP's Building a More Perfect Union project, young people in several communities across the country had the opportunity to discover for themselves a hidden history in their communities and, empowered by that knowledge and the tools and resources to uncover it, relay that history to others, from teachers to grandparents to national conference attendees.

The New York City Writing Project (NYCWP) aimed to surface the untold history of Van Cortlandt Park, a magnificent park in the Bronx known for its many hiking and walking trails and recreational facilities. Less known is the fact that the park sits on what was once a plantation and that enclosed within the park is the burial ground of enslaved people. Through a project entitled "A More Perfect Bronx History," high school students made this hidden history known to their peers, teachers, and the public. They interviewed and conversed with park attendees, developed digital artifacts, and presented their work at a conference at nearby Lehman College.

When visiting the burial ground for the first time, the students were shocked by the lack of attention it had received. They noted that the signage felt temporary and was not in keeping with what they saw at other cemeteries, including the nearby Kingsbridge Cemetery, also inside the park's grounds. The students considered how they could improve the site, marking it as sacred ground while educating park visitors, students, and teachers about the place and history.

"The nature of the history of U.S. slavery is incomplete, imperfect and inaccurate," said NYC Writing Project Director Jane Kehoe-Higgins. "We learned that we needed to gather knowledge in ways that did not adhere to the traditional processes of academic research and reporting. We learned that we needed to be open to each encounter and find ways to synthesize knowledge as we picked up morsels of information from each person we spoke with while following the paths of both enslaved Africans and free Blacks." The students involved in this project imagined a new future for a lost history and made their vision a reality.

At the Boston Writing Project, students and teachers from area schools responded to the question "What does it mean to be Black in Boston today?" As part of a larger city project, "Writing Boston's Future," they learned together by delving into the past in order to better understand the present in Boston's Museum of African American History. They created artifacts that ranged from paintings to digital photo collages, which were presented during a public event at the museum and are now part of the archives. The group was also invited to showcase their work during the NAACP's 114th annual convention in Boston.

In many cases, the students began the project unaware of the museum's existence. By the end, though, they not only knew about it, but were invested in it. Leaders from the Boston Writing Project recount that one student's grandfather praised the entire endeavor, saying that his granddaughter was "working harder this summer than she did all during the school year" and talking to her family about their past experiences in Boston. Then he added: "When can people from my generation learn more about this history that we were never taught in schools? I'm hungry to learn about us!" Another student wrote: "The fact that we can continue to learn from the Museum and the history it has to offer excites me," while another said, "I feel pretty good—not gonna lie. I feel fulfilled and somewhat accomplished!"

And isn't that what Adam Gopnik was getting at when he distinguished between achievement and accomplishment?

Across these projects and many others, student writers were invited into ongoing conversations about the places where they lived.

They were asked to engage in a conversation about a more complex, nuanced history of that place than they may have experienced in school history class, but beyond that, *they* were invited to decide what should be done with that knowledge, how it should be put to use. Then they created resources, lessons, and events that could change the perception of their communities. These student writers were seen as capable and competent, and they provided the means and opportunity to make something that could change the world they live in, making them agents of change. But more importantly, the knowledge that their research and writing mattered, that it would actually be read and maybe acted upon, was a motivator to work hard, distinguish information from misinformation, and work to be understood. By doing real work, rather than rote work, they claimed their own agency as writers and creators.

AUTHORS' NOTE

We know that young writers live in a complex world and face real threats to their mental and physical health and to the world in which they live. At the same time, they generally attend schools that have strived for over a decade to break learning into discrete parts and measurable outcomes, leading to more and more efforts to measure student learning and growth as a series of "ephemeral achievements." We seem to be stuck in a system that does not support writerly growth, and this fact makes us at best frustrated, and mostly sad.

However, when students participate in the larger world as thinkers, writers, and change agents, they become more involved in and take more responsibility for their own learning and know themselves to be agentive human beings. These are the accomplishments at the heart of writing, especially in a complex, AI-driven world, and these are the experiences that we want to create in individual classrooms and across schools. Every time we read about teachers and students extending the boundaries of their classrooms, we get a little giddy. Writing the examples in this chapter made us happy in a way that we desperately needed as we navigated the world's challenges, our individual jobs, personal commitments, and all of the other distracting things that delayed our writing progress. The stories inspired us, and we hope they inspire you to extend the classroom walls.

CHAPTER 5

Writing (and Writing Teachers) Still Matter

Practices for Leading and Learning

At Rutgers University in 1975, professor and writing researcher Janet Emig scheduled a series of visiting lecturers on teaching writing—James Britton, Don Graves, Don Murray, Lee Odell, Mina Shaughnessy. This was my first introduction to a whole community of writers, writing researchers and writing teachers. I'll be forever indebted to those titans of writing pedagogy.
—Steve Zemelman, North Eastern University

> Writing is for everyone, at every level of skill, from every background and lifestyle.
>
> —Jesus Vedoya Renteria, Hanaford West High School

Networking, which once felt dreadful and performative, transformed into something genuine. I no longer isolate when problems arise; instead, I know exactly who I can reach out to, trust their advice, and count on being respected and valued as a person. There are so many humans that I am entirely grateful. They took a chance on me, gave me the time and space, and I am humbled.
—Lisa Gusewelle, McLean Family Resource Center

> In addition to heartfelt encouragement and support, my professional learning mates offer thoughtful critique. But what feeds me most is listening. We are friends. Friends to laugh with, friends to write with, friends who show me, again and again, that I belong as a writer.
>
> —Patricia Murray, Husson University

Up to this point, we as the authors have intentionally written in the third person, sharing our "royal we" reflections only at the end of each chapter. We have argued that writing is a rich, complex, and deeply fascinating human act, and teachers are central in developing young writers' capacity. Throughout the book, we have introduced amazing teachers and promising practices. We also looked at technological developments like AI that are challenging the field of writing instruction by redefining what writing is and how writers create in contemporary times. Our decision to write with an academic voice helped us to situate what research on writing and writing instruction has revealed over time. Third person kept the "us" in the background, relegated to authors' notes of short reflections.

But this chapter is our letter of invitation to you to join us more deeply in the work of reflection, in the challenge of leadership, and in the admirable call of being a teacher of writing in community. In recent years, many teachers have come to expect "just in time" professional learning—the ability to find the answer to any teaching question, the materials for any lesson, the solution to any behavioral problem—whenever they need it. Listservs like the Gates Foundation's Teacher2Teacher send practical tips into a teacher's inbox every Friday. Teachers Pay Teachers allows anyone to pay a few dollars for a complete classroom lesson sequence, including student handouts and teacher PowerPoints. Generative AI can create differentiated lesson plans in less than a minute. In such a wealth of information, one might wonder whether NWP's approach is necessary. The NWP model, though, offers more than information, more than decontextualized tips for success, more than lesson plans. The social practices that undergird NWP's community of practice provide an inquiry stance and a framework for professional discernment that you can share with your colleagues as part of a lifelong learning and teaching community. Learning to be a better writing teacher is a lifelong pursuit; it is one filled with experimentation, creativity, and joy; great colleagues; and lifelong friends.

We want you to know that you already have everything you need for a lifetime of learning with and from your students, and that there's plenty of intrepid and curious colleagues to keep you company along the way. The NWP has long believed in "teachers teaching teachers," practitioners at all levels working together *as* practitioners to inquire into practice. We also believe that knowledge about the teaching of writing comes from many sources:

theory and research, the analysis of practice, and the experience of writing. This chapter embodies those values of the National Writing Project and provides you with a framework for moving forward in your professional learning and leadership.

REFLECTION POINT: YOU ALREADY HAVE EVERYTHING YOU NEED TO KEEP LEARNING ABOUT WRITING AND TEACHING WRITING

The design of the first Invitational Summer Institute of the National Writing Project in 1974 was built on a foundational idea. James Gray believed, "If we want to know about teaching writing, we should find great teachers and see what they do." By bringing together a group of talented teachers and examining what they did and how they knew what to do, Gray realized that teachers' knowledge about teaching writing was shaped by multiple sources—their own experiences as writers, the instruction they had received, their classroom practice, and the research they engaged with.

NWP continues to believe that the best teachers draw on all these ways of knowing. Professional learning for writing teachers, therefore, should include opportunities to write, to experience the practices of effective teachers, to read and discuss current research, and to reflect deeply on their own practice. Every teacher can implement practices to continue their learning as a teacher of writing.

Practice #1: Be a Writer

To teach writing well, teachers must write. By this we don't mean that every teacher needs to become a published author (although you can). We mean that teachers should engage in some regular writing practice.

Being a writer means engaging regularly in the act of composing—whether journaling, blogging, drafting articles, or experimenting with poetry—and reflecting on one's own process. It involves recognizing that writing is not simply transcription but an act of discovery. As Joan Didion (2021) once wrote, "I write entirely to find out what I am thinking." There is no better way to destabilize the myths that we named in Chapter 2 than to experience for yourself how writers make countless choices as they work—choosing words, shaping sentences, rethinking ideas—and how through those choices, they often uncover new understandings, new things they want to say.

Being a writer also means accepting that writing is rarely linear. Many teachers who are writers have commented how they now understand that the thing they used to present as "the writing process" rarely moves neatly from one step to another, but instead often recursively moves back and forth and through many ways of looking at and thinking about a piece of writing. People who write with other people begin to know that there are some things that most writers do, but that those writers might do those same things in different ways, and that there are some things that are idiosyncratic to each writer.

As you write, you may find yourself organizing your thoughts before drafting in diverse ways, by drawing or mapping or outlining and more. While anyone who wants to write something will eventually have to draft their piece, some people will begin at the beginning and write through to the end, while others always write their introduction last, after they see what they have actually written. Some writers start with "just the basics" in a first draft to see if they feel they are on the right track, while others will free-write pages and pages, knowing that half of what they put down will later be cut. It doesn't matter what your process is. Just write.

Why It Matters

Regularly writing, learning how you write, facing the myriad of decisions it takes to put the just right word in the just right place, helps you to see that there is more than one way through the process; it promotes empathy for student writers who find themselves in a stuck place; and it reduces your own desire to make the process frictionless for your students. Being a teacher who writes and is willing to share your process, your own drafts, and your own work means being able to meet students in your classroom writer-to-writer.

When teachers write, they deepen their understanding of what writing truly is: a complex, often messy process of thinking and rethinking. Beyond what teachers-who-write learn about writing, Lieberman and Freidrich also show that teacher writers begin to see teaching itself as a complex set of decisions, taking more "authority" of the teaching and learning that happens in their classrooms (Lieberman & Freidrich 2010). Writing regularly helps teachers:

- Recognize that there are many valid ways to approach writing.
- Build empathy for students who struggle or feel "stuck."
- Resist the urge to make writing frictionless for students, instead guiding them through productive struggle.
- Develop a richer sense of what feedback, revision, and audience mean in practice.
- Cultivate a classroom culture where writing is shared, discussed, and seen as a living, evolving act.

How to Do It

- **Write regularly.** Carve out 10 minutes at the beginning or end of your teaching day to write. Reflect on your classroom, your life, or a topic you care about. Most importantly, just write.
- **Write with colleagues.** Start a teacher writing group that meets weekly or monthly. The group might simply hold space for writing together or share and respond to one another's work.
- **Write about teaching.** Reflective writing can clarify what you value as an educator and help you identify patterns in your practice.
- **Write beyond teaching.** Try creative writing, personal essays, or professional articles. Expanding your writing identity nurtures confidence and perspective.
- **Join existing writing communities.**
    - **National Writing Project's Write Out:** Each year the National Writing Project offers a 2-week event called Write Out where folks are invited to go outside and write. While the program offers lots of prompts and ideas about how you might engage in writing outdoors, really all that's required to participate is going outside and writing.
    - **Ethical ELA:** Sarah Donovan, writing project leader at the Oklahoma State University Writing Project, hosts a weekly blog, Ethical ELA, which began in 2015 as a space to process everyday teaching experiences in the ELA classroom. The mission has expanded to serve the teachers who come to the space to discover how ELA can nurture the hearts and minds of teachers

and the students they serve. With over 800,000 views and 200,000 visitors from across the world, Ethical ELA persists because teachers contribute, nurture, and shape this space. It is public, free of advertisements, memberships, and sponsorships. Ethical ELA offers monthly writing PD and occasional writing challenges/invitations like Verselove. Verselove takes place in April and invites participants to read and write poems every day during poetry month.
    - » **Writers Who Care:** Founded by members of the Commission on Writing Teacher Education of the English Language Arts Teacher Educator conference of NCTE (many of whom were also NWP-affiliated), the Writers Who Care blog advocates for effective writing instruction and welcomes writing about classroom practice from teachers.
- **Create your own challenges.** Invite students or colleagues to join you in a 30-day journaling challenge or a "write every day for a week" experiment.
- **Share your process.** Let students see your drafts, your revisions, and your thinking aloud as a writer. This transparency models authenticity and persistence.

Writing regularly—alone and with others—will not only strengthen your own voice but also transform how you teach, respond to, and nurture the writers in your classroom.

Practice #2: Learn From Research

Since the very first summer institute of the Bay Area Writing Project, the Writing Project has designed learning opportunities for teachers that include reading the latest theory and research along with analyzing practice and writing. In the early years, there was much less research and theory to read! In the past 50 years, research on writing has exploded. But learning from research doesn't necessarily mean keeping up with every publication in every academic journal. It can also mean participating in a book study with colleagues in professional learning communities, listening to interviews and podcasts, and subscribing to teaching-focused journals from professional organizations. The same explosion of research that can make learning from research so overwhelming is responsible for whole new genres of summaries, explainers, and author talks conducted over Zoom that make the connections between research and practice.

Part of what makes learning from research so enjoyable at NWP institutes and events is that it is not done alone. All the same activities that we might use in our classrooms with students—reading circles, reflective conversations, jigsaws, and so on—can work with us teachers as well. And when learning from research is embedded in school-based learning communities, many systems and institutions will allow time for teachers to meet during professional development days.

Why It Matters

Teachers who stay connected to research are better positioned to make informed decisions and to advocate for best practices in their schools. It is difficult for teachers to advocate for the best practices in teaching—or to counter arguments against researched practice—if they don't make consuming and reflecting on research a regular part of their ongoing professional learning.

Engaging with research helps teachers:

- Stay current on new perspectives, evidence, and innovations in literacy and writing instruction.
- Bridge the gap between theory and practice by adapting research for their own classrooms.
- Strengthen their credibility as professionals who can explain and justify instructional choices.
- Cultivate curiosity and lifelong learning within their teaching communities.

How to Do It

- **Subscribe to practitioner-friendly journals** such as *The Reading Teacher, English Journal,* or *Voices From the Middle* to keep up with accessible, classroom-focused research.
- **Join professional organizations** like NCTE or the National Writing Project to access research-based resources and conversations.

- **Form or join a professional learning community (PLC)** that explores both classroom data and research on shared problems of practice.
- **Try informal learning formats**, such as the South Coast Writing Project's One Beer Professional Reading Group—read one article and meet at a pub to discuss it for exactly as long as it takes to drink one beer.
- **Participate in online communities** like NWP's Write Now Teacher Studio, which hosts ongoing groups such as:
    - » Jonathan Marine's James Moffett Study Group, where teachers meet monthly to discuss 5–8 pages of a seminal text.
    - » Writers and Robots, an open streaming platform where educators post and discuss resources related to teaching with generative AI.
- **Expand what it means to read.** Subscribe to a podcast like *The Cult of Pedagogy* or *Children and Screens*.

Practice #3: Study Your Own Teaching Practice

Studying your own teaching practice means approaching your classroom as a site of inquiry. It's about being curious about what happens in your teaching, why it happens, and how you can learn from it. Teacher researchers systematically investigate their practice through observation, documentation, reflection, and collaboration to improve both student learning and their own instructional decisions.

Cindy Ballenger, in *Teaching IS Inquiry* (2025), identified three values of inquiring teachers (curiosity, collegiality, and reflection) and three core practices: find a focus, stop time, and talk with colleagues. Curious teachers do not assume that if something "didn't work" it must be because there is something "wrong" with the student. Rather, they come to view students who aren't learning in step with others as "puzzling" and to ask questions about how that student is making sense in a way that is different from others. A curious teacher seeks to figure out what REALLY works in their instruction, for whom, and why. Once there is a puzzle to focus on, a teacher has to have some way to "stop time," in other words, to save some of the puzzling evidence of learning to come back to out of the continually moving stream that a classroom is. Recording classroom conversations to be able to listen to later or taking notes are two time-tested ways that teachers who want to make sense of their classrooms "stop time" so that they can relisten or in other ways return to the scene later.

Reflection, alone or with colleagues, helps us to see our practice more clearly, to understand it more deeply, and to explain it to others who are curious about and/or want to learn from what they see us doing. Reflection can happen in informal writing, such as journaling, or in conversation with colleagues.

All of this work helps teachers to be researchers, engaging in inquiry that supports—or refutes—their gut decisions. This kind of deep reflective practice will make you stop, question, and seek feedback (talk) with colleagues.

Why It Matters

Teaching can easily feel, as one of our former students once said, like "one damn thing after another." Especially in the early years of teaching, or within chaotic systems, it's easy to move from one task to the next without deep reflection on the decisions we make, our reasons for doing those things, and the learning we can take from them.

As Anne Whitney suggests in *Teaching Writers to Reflect* (2019), reflection is what transforms students' experiences into learning. The same holds true for teachers: Systematic reflection turns classroom moments into professional insight. In order to have continuity from year to year, to see how we are able to grow and change, and to feel some efficacy in the world of school, it is important that we develop ways to learn from our own practice.

Studying your own practice helps teachers:

- Transform daily experience into professional learning.
- Identify what truly works in instruction—and for whom.
- Develop a sense of agency, continuity, and purpose across years.
- Build reflective habits that make teaching more intentional and sustainable.
- Contribute to the wider profession by sharing findings with others.

How to Do It

- **Adopt a curious stance.** When something doesn't work, don't assume it's a student problem—treat it as a puzzle.

Ask, "What might be happening here?" or "How is this student making sense differently from others?"

- **Find a focus.** Identify a single question or problem of practice you want to understand better (e.g., "How does feedback timing affect revision depth?").
- **Stop time.** Collect classroom artifacts—student writing, notes, or recordings—that let you return later to moments of learning or confusion.
- **Talk with colleagues.** Collaborate with peers to analyze classroom moments and generate new interpretations.
- **Write reflectively.** Keep a teaching journal or blog to document insights, patterns, and surprises over time.
- **Share your learning.** Present at a staff meeting, write a short reflection for a newsletter, or post in an online teacher researcher community.

REFLECTION POINT: YOU DON'T HAVE TO GO IT ALONE

An old adage tells us that if we want to go fast, we should go alone, but if we want to go far we should go together. This may be truer for those in the teaching profession than in any other. Teaching can be a surprisingly lonely endeavor, especially in the United States. Although teachers work in buildings full of children and colleagues, they often work in isolation, solely responsible for the learning, health, and well-being of the young people in their classrooms. Few U.S. schools are organized with adequate time for teachers to collaborate or solve the problems of work together. Data on teacher retention show that more than half of those who enter the profession leave within their first 5 years.

James Gray recognized that despite the negative public discourse about teachers, his experiences of his teaching colleagues as smart, caring, and curious people informed his decision to bring teachers together in ways that featured collaboration, leadership, and advocacy. NWP was founded to make teachers the center of the work, positioning them not primarily as learners, but as a community of practice with the capacity and responsibility to collaborate, lead, and advocate. Whether Gray understood this in 1974 or came to see it over time, he realized that teachers with strong professional networks could address day-to-day challenges, take on new problems, and not only remain in the profession but also find joy and fulfillment throughout their careers. Over its history, much has been written about the power of networked learning and its impact on teachers inside the National Writing Project. This is notably studied in *Inside the National Writing Project* (Lieberman & Wood, 2002).

Kira Baker-Doyle (2011) has studied the impact of networks on new teachers' professional lives. Drawing on social network theory, she distinguishes between two key types of teacher networks: *intentional professional networks* and *networks of diverse professional allies.* Teachers' intentional professional networks are primarily local—colleagues they "select to collaborate and interact with to solve professional problems" (p. 22). These networks help teachers "navigate the norms of their schools, establish their status and professional identity, solve everyday problems, and feel more confident about their work" (p. 22). Networks of diverse professional allies, by contrast, often include community members (parents, students, and others) who "provide new ideas, foster innovation, and, for the teachers, a deeper sense of engagement with students and their curriculum" (p. 58).

While these distinctions are not rigid, Baker-Doyle's framework helps clarify the range of opportunities networks can offer: finding well-matched colleagues, engaging with people who bring innovative perspectives, and cultivating a social context that sustains deep engagement with the intellectual and practical challenges of teaching. Such networks make teaching a long-term, meaningful pursuit worthy of sustained energy and attention.

For many teachers who have spent their professional lives involved with NWP, the local and national NWP networks provide both kinds of support: collaborating on the day-to-day work of teaching and learning while also engaging with new ideas and shared problems of practice. "Going together" has become the norm, shaping how teachers write, learn, lead, and advocate—for one another and for what they know to be best for their students and their profession. You have a network available to you, and you have the power to create your own.

Practice #4: Collaborate on the Day-to-Day Questions

Collaborating on the day-to-day questions of teaching means working with colleagues to make classroom practice public, to share what works, and to study together the ongoing challenges of teaching and learning. It's about recognizing that teaching is complex, context-dependent work and that no one teacher, curriculum, or policy can capture all the wisdom needed to meet the diverse needs of students.

NWP's model of professional learning embodies this approach: Teachers learn *with and from* one another by sharing their practices, testing ideas, and reflecting collaboratively. Professional expertise is not imported from outside, but cultivated and distributed within a community of teacher leaders.

Why It Matters

In recent years there has been a significant devaluation of the expertise of teachers, as can be seen in policies, practices, and instructional resources that strive to be "teacher-proof." This attitude belies the complexity of teaching, focusing on *what* is being taught with very little attention paid to the context of the teaching or the students in the classroom.

Yet research tells us that teachers take in more information and make more decisions in a day than air traffic controllers. The same curricular materials will look and feel different in the hands of an experienced teacher than a novice one; in a classroom of 40 students versus 20; in a classroom of students who speak a single language than in a multilingual classroom. NWP's model of professional learning centers the expertise of classroom teachers by inviting them (and us) to learn from real experiences and to make teaching practice public so that others may learn from it as well.

Collaborative inquiry restores and sustains the professional dignity of teaching. It helps teachers:

- Recognize and value their own expertise as central to improving education.
- Learn from diverse contexts, seeing how similar lessons unfold differently depending on students, setting, and experience.
- Break down isolation by creating networks of shared inquiry.
- Improve instruction through feedback, reflection, and co-analysis of student learning.
- Build professional cultures where experimentation and learning are celebrated rather than penalized.

As Marilyn Cochran-Smith and Susan Lytle document (2009), when teachers collaborate on real classroom questions, they elevate the practice of teaching from private work to shared professional knowledge.

How to Do It

- **Engage in lesson study.** Work with a colleague—in your school or in a broader network—to collaboratively design, teach, and analyze a lesson. Visit one another's classrooms if possible, or videoconference in to talk to your colleagues' students. Reflect on the same lesson enacted in different contexts and study the resulting student work together.
- **Build ongoing collaborative structures.** Create standing PLCs or inquiry groups that meet regularly to examine classroom questions such as "How do we help students sustain revision?" or "How do we support multilingual writers in workshop discussions?" Collect data from your classroom to share with your colleagues.

Practice #5: Share New Ideas

Sharing new ideas means engaging with innovation—whether it emerges from new research, new policies, or unexpected disruptions—and doing so in community. It involves teachers collaborating to understand what's new, testing ideas in real classrooms, and contributing their discoveries back to the field. NWP has been, and continues to be, a leader when disruptions in writing practice or the teaching of writing occur.

For instance, the Common Core State Standards (CCSS) originated from a state-led effort by the National Governors Association (NGA) and the Council of Chief State School Officers (CCSSO) to establish consistent, rigorous academic expectations for K–12 students. Development began in 2009, and the standards were released in Spring 2010. The initiative aimed to prepare students for college and careers by addressing inconsistencies in state standards and the desire for American students to compete globally. In the area of writing, CCSS pushed schools and teachers to largely abandon narrative writing, especially in the middle and high school grades, in favor of teaching argument and informational writing. The quick adoption of the CCSS left many teachers feeling unprepared to teach these modes of writing. The National Writing Project organized teachers to write, learn and lead together, developing NWP's College, Career, and Community Writers Program (C3WP), a highly successful professional learning program that supported teachers to become better at teaching argument writing.

NWP teacher leaders developed theories and practices for teaching argument writing and worked with groups of teachers to study new lessons on aspects of teaching argument writing such as creating nuanced claims, making moves with evidence, and writing an op-ed. Leaders in the program also developed a formative assessment tool, the Using Sources Tool, that focuses teachers' review of student work on the aspects of argument writing that they are teaching.

Likewise, when generative AI arrived in classrooms in 2022, the NWP network once again demonstrated how teachers share and develop new ideas in the face of disruption. Much of the talk around generative AI, especially early on, seemed driven by fear, for example, "How will we stop students from cheating?" or "Is this the end of writing instruction?" Within the National Writing Project network, local and cross-site subnetworks began to approach the question of AI with curiosity. Some writing project sites, like Red River Valley in North Dakota, added new books to their Invitational Leadership Institutes in order to read and learn together about AI, and to design classroom experiments in its use as a tool for learning. At the Midwest directors' retreat in the spring of 2024, five sites organized themselves into a collective effort to do the same thing, creating local site networks of teacher researchers who were also part of a larger network that met regularly to learn from one another's work.

In New York City, Paul Allison refocused his Teachers Teaching Teachers (TTT) network, an informal group of colleagues spread across the nation, to focus completely on the use of generative AI in the classroom. TTT, which has been an ongoing drop-in network of educators interested in technology who have met once a week online for more than a decade, began organizing themselves to learn about what was possible in classrooms using generative AI. At Drew University in New Jersey, the site organized what has become an annual symposium to bring teachers together to have critical conversations about GenAI and writing. The key here is that a network of teachers came together to write, learn, and lead, and you can do this, too.

Why It Matters

Education is dynamic. New standards, technologies, and social realities continually reshape classrooms. Facing the challenges, working collaboratively and across networks to solve problems, and sharing learning are keys to successful writing instruction.

By working together to explore and test new ideas, teachers:

- Transform uncertainty into professional learning and innovation.
- Build capacity to respond thoughtfully to change—whether prompted by policy, technology, or community shifts.
- Develop and refine classroom-tested practices that address emerging challenges.
- Strengthen professional agency, ensuring that teachers shape educational change rather than being shaped by it.
- Model curiosity, adaptability, and reflective learning for students.

When teachers jump in, experiment, and share new ideas, they generate knowledge that drives the profession forward.

How to Do It

- **Share your successful lessons and units.** Whether locally or at a national conference, seek opportunities to share your practice, gather feedback, and reflect. Implement changes based on what you learn.
- **Respond to disruptions with curiosity, not fear.** Every new threat is an opportunity. Seek the affordances (benefits) and weigh the challenges (limitations).
- **Build cross-site learning networks.** Form a community of teacher researchers who plan to share classroom experiments and meet regularly to learn from one another's findings. If you don't have a local writing project network to find your people, connect with others on the Write Now Teacher Studio.
- **Leverage longstanding communities.** The Teachers Teaching Teachers (TTT) network is a digital space that invites teachers to deepen their understanding.

- **Document and share your findings.** Make the insights that emerge from collaboration public—through staff meetings, local conferences, blogs, or NWP networks—so that your learning benefits a wider community. If possible, partner with a university colleague to write up your findings for research journals.

A FINAL NOTE

Teaching writing is hard. There is not an easy plan that says, "here's what you do." But there is a way for you to go about figuring it out. You have the tools:

1. Be a writer.
2. Learn from research.
3. Study your own teaching practice.
4. Collaborate on the day-to-day questions.
5. Share new ideas.

And you have the community.

In the introduction to her book *Thrive* (2014), Meenoo Rami, a teacher consultant for the Philadelphia Writing Project, describes feeling isolated in her early days as a teacher, isolation that she attributes to the difficulties of learning to be a good teacher, weariness, and often feeling like a failure. She then goes on to say:

> Slowly, I discovered my own power to find meaning, solve complex problems, and make meaningful connections that inspire me to this very day. This slow evolution as an empowered teacher happened because of a few very specific experiences: I joined communities like the National Writing Project and National Council for Teachers of English. I met mentors . . . , and I started contributing to my field by starting conversations about teaching and learning . . . These experiences helped me feel less alone and armed me with a variety of new tools and ideas that helped my students and let me see my practice with new eyes. . . . The success I have experienced in my brief career is not accidental. What I have done is ask for help relentlessly; I have begged, borrowed, and stolen great ideas from teachers in my professional network. Fearlessly, I have tried new ideas. I have trusted my

> students to take on challenging and meaningful work that resonates with their personal interests, investments, and inquiries. (p. xvii)

Meenoo has given back to the profession, to our community, as much as she has taken, sharing ideas freely, presenting at conferences, and writing about her work. As teacher leaders and longtime Writing Project Teacher Consultants, the authors of this book claim paths into the heart of the profession that are all unique, but also share many similarities with the story Meenoo tells.

We invite you to join us. Our wish for you, reader, is that you find your own network, your own passions, and your own intellectual pursuits within the field of teaching writing. We believe that you will find no end of intellectual questions, mysterious students, and exceptional fellow travelers if you approach teaching this way. And we know from long and deep experience that our shared work in this complex endeavor will be improved through your work and explorations.

Writing Will Continue to Matter

For more than 5 decades, NWP has insisted that writing matters—for thinking, for identity, for community, for agency. Even as the tools of writing evolve, fundamental truths about writing remain:

- Writing is a way for humans to make meaning.
- Writing is linked to identity and belonging.
- Writers grow through practice, feedback, and reflection in community.
- Writing is a mode of participation in public life.

Technologies will continue to change and make demands on teachers' practice, but amplifying the human processes of writing and the ongoing growth of young people should remain at the forefront of what writing teachers do. We believe teachers can make writing matter, even in an age of AI.

Imagine this snapshot, co-authored with GenAI, of an AI-enhanced writing studio 10 years into the future:

> Writers step into a classroom that feels less like a room and more like a creative ecosystem—a studio, lab, and publishing house woven together. The hum is unmistakable: quiet concentration from writers drafting in notebooks that sync their handwritten words to digital spaces; bursts of collaborative energy around screens where ideas are being shaped, questioned, and tested.
>
> Each student begins with an AI-supported writing notebook, a hybrid journal that blends pen strokes with machine-generated nudges. A handwritten line becomes a prompt for reflection: "What's the tension here?" or "Whose perspective hasn't been heard yet?" Instead of correcting or completing their writing, the AI acts like a curious peer, a thinking partner that pushes rather than replaces human reasoning.

> Across the room, students curate their own digital writing hubs that look like personal sites where drafts, poems, multimedia pieces, and reflections grow into a living portfolio. AI tools quietly organize and link their work, pairing essays with emerging themes, generating visuals that match tone and mood, and assembling small constellations of their ideas over time.
>
> Clusters of students gather around collaborative screens, co-authoring pieces for the class's online magazine. AI helps manage the workflow by suggesting alternative structures, surfacing contradictions, or analyzing the emotional arc of a piece, but the creative and editorial authority stays firmly with the writers. Their work is published to real audiences: families, other classrooms, community members, or partner schools around the world. Writers ask their human teacher guide for insight, to help them solve problems or curate resources, or for a human take on their ideas and creations.
>
> In another corner, VR headsets hang beside shelves of novels. Students slip into virtual spaces inspired by the texts they're studying—not to escape the world of the book, but to experience it more deeply. They collect sensory details, walk the terrain of a scene, or record notes for a narrative they'll later craft. Nearby, others design branching stories in game-writing tools, testing how choices shape meaning.
>
> Everything students create—notes, drafts, storyboards, videos, reflections—flows into a living portfolio powered by analytics that illuminate growth. Their digital gardens help them to connect ideas, learn publicly, and constantly revise their thinking. Teachers see patterns in voice, structure, risk-taking, and revision, helping them guide writers with precision and care.

It is a learning space overflowing with possibility. The tools are new, the technologies evolving, but the heartbeat is familiar: a community of writers learning, experimenting, imagining, and publishing together. In this future, students write, compose, design, and curate. AI partners push their thinking. Publishing is participatory, portfolios are living ecosystems, and writing is multimodal and expansive, focused on process over product. The writer in this ecosystem is not only a composer of text but a sense-maker, designer, and collaborator—with and through machines and humans alike. Teachers work to make sure that regardless of the tools, the classroom maintains a desirable difficulty.

In just a few years from the publication of this book, this future may be a reality in some classrooms. Or it may not describe what exists at all, or what exists for the few, not the many. At this point in time, however, teachers of writing must ask: Is this the future we want? If not, what does the future we want look like?

If we have motivated you to gather with colleagues in order to ask questions about writing and the teaching of writing, we leave you with some contemplative questions to guide you in creating the writing classrooms of the future:

- What do writers gain if AI becomes a thinking partner?
- What do writers lose if human imagination, struggle, and community are not foregrounded?
- How do writers maintain agency in a space where machines generate content effortlessly?
- How do we ensure that writers are given the opportunity to pursue accomplishment, not just achievement?
- How do all writers, not just privileged ones, access the ability to write, publish, and lead in a digital, AI-enhanced world?
- How are NWP values present, including writing as a social process, teacher knowledge and leadership, writing for real work, and equity and access?

Teaching writing is hard work, full of challenges. No matter the time, place, or technologies, there will be struggles. No future is guaranteed. At the center of any future worth building is the human writer—their agency, imagination, and voice. Building an ecosystem where AI deepens thinking, expands creativity, and opens doors for writers who have often been overlooked requires intentionality and an unwavering commitment to equity.

The next era of writing is unfolding. If writing still matters—and it does—then the future of writing matters even more. If young people are at the center—and they must be—then the writing classroom, whatever form it takes, will remain a place of power, possibility, and hope.

We invite you to keep thinking about why writing matters and share your responses with the National Writing Project (nwp.org.).

References

ACT. (2016). *The condition of college and career readiness 2016*. ACT, Inc.

Baker-Doyle, K. (2011). *The networked teacher: How new teachers build social networks for professional support*. Teachers College Press.

Baker-Bell, A. (2020). *Linguistic justice: Black language, literacy, identity, and pedagogy*. Routledge.

Ballenger, C. (2025). *Teaching IS inquiry: Observation and reflection as the heart of practice*. Teachers College Press.

Baron, N. S. (2008). *Always on: Language in an online and mobile world*. Oxford University Press.

Bazerman, C. (1988). *Shaping written knowledge: The genre and activity of the experimental article in science*. University of Wisconsin Press.

Beaufort, A. (2007). *College writing and beyond: A new framework for university writing instruction*. Utah State University Press.

Bereiter, C., & Scardamalia, M. (1987). *The psychology of written composition*. Lawrence Erlbaum Associates.

Bjork, R. A. (1994). Memory and metamemory considerations in the training of human beings. In J. Metcalfe & A. Shimamura (Eds.), *Metacognition: Knowing about knowing* (pp. 185–205). MIT Press.

Braddock, R., Lloyd-Jones, R., & Schoer, L. (1963). *Research in written composition*. National Council of Teachers of English.

Campbell, K., & Latimer, K. (2012). *Beyond the five paragraph essay*. Routledge.

Carr, N. (2010). *The shallows: What the Internet is doing to our brains*. W. W. Norton & Company.

Caufield, M., & Wineburg, S. (2023). *Verified: How to think straight, get duped less, and make better decisions about what to believe online*. University of Chicago Press.

Cochran-Smith, M., & Lytle, S. (2009). *Inquiry as stance: Practitioner research for the next generation*. Teachers College Press.

Connected Learning Alliance. (n.d.). *What is connected learning?* Author. https://connectedlearning.org/what-is-connected-learning/

Cope, B., & Kalantzis, M. (2009). "Multiliteracies": New literacies, new learning. *Pedagogies: An International Journal, 4*(3), 164–195. https://doi.org/10.1080/15544800903076044

Didion, J. (2021). "Why I Write." In *Let Me Tell You What I Mean* (pp. 3–18). Alfred A. Knopf.

Early, J. (2022). *Next generation genres: Teaching writing for civic and academic engagement.* Norton Professional Books.

Emig, J. (1971). *The composing process of twelfth graders.* National Council of Teachers of English.

Epstein, D. (2025). A risk of cognitive convenience. *Range Widely.* https://davidepstein.substack.com/p/a-risk-of-cognitive-convenience

Fecho, B. (2011). *Writing in the dialogical classroom: Students and teachers responding to the texts of their lives.* National Council of Teachers of English.

Feldgus, E., & Cardonick, I. (1999). *Kid writing: A systematic approach to phonics, journals, and writing workshop.* Wright Group/McGraw Hill.

Fleischer, C., & Andrew-Vaughan, S. (2009). *Writing outside your comfort zone: Helping students navigate unfamiliar genres.* Heinemann.

Flower, L. (1979). Writer-based prose: A cognitive basis for problems in writing. *College English, 41*(1), 19–37. https://doi.org/10.2307/376357

Flower, L., & Hayes, J. R. (1981). A cognitive process theory of writing. *College Composition and Communication, 32*(4), 365–387. https://doi.org/10.2307/356600

Freedman, S.W. (1987). *Response to student writing* [Research Report 23]. National Council of Teachers of English.

Garcia, A. (2019). Foreword. In Turner, K. H. (Ed.), *The ethics of digital literacy: Developing knowledge and skills across grade levels* (xiii-xv). Rowman & Littlefield.

Gere, A. R. (1987). *Writing groups: History, theory, and implications.* Southern Illinois University Press.

Gopnik, A. (2023). *The real work: On the mystery of mastery.* Liveright.

Gort, M., Zapata, A., Seltzer, K., & Gómez, M. (Eds). (2025). *Translanguaging perspectives on writing development and pedagogy: Learning from findings across teaching and learning contexts.* Emerald Publishing.

Graham, S. (2018). A revised writer(s)-within-community model of writing. *Educational Psychologist, 53*(4), 258–279. https://doi.org/10.1080/00461520.2018.1481406

Graham, S., & Perin, D. (2007). A meta-analysis of writing instruction for adolescent students. *Journal of Educational Psychology, 99*(3), 445–476. https://doi.org/10.1037/0022-0663.99.3.445

Haidt, J. (2024). *The anxious generation: How the great rewiring of childhood is causing an epidemic of mental illness.* Penguin Press.

Harris, K., Graham, S., & Mason, L. H. (2006). Improving the writing, knowledge, and motivation of struggling young writers: Effects of self-regulated strategy development with and without peer support. *American Educational Research Journal, 43*(2), 295–340.

Hicks, T., & Turner, K. H. (2026). Enhancing instruction with the intentional integration of digital literacies. In J. Castek, J. Coiro, E. Forzani, C. Kiili, M. Schira-Hagerman, & Sparks, J. R. (Eds.), *International handbook of research in digital literacies* [Forthcoming]. Routledge.

Hicks, T., & Turner, K. H. (2025). *Teaching writing in the age of AI: Strategies for teachers of secondary students*. Solution Tree.

Hicks, T., Turner, K. H., & Stratton, J. (2013). Reimagining a writer's process through digital storytelling. *LEARNing Landscapes, 6*(2), 167–183. https://doi.org/10.36510/learnland.v6i2.611

Hillocks, G. Jr. (1986). *Research on written composition: New directions for teaching*. National Conference on Research in English.

Hillocks, G. Jr. (1995). *Teaching writing as reflective practice*. Teachers College Press.

Hillocks, G. (2002). *The testing trap: How state writing assessments control learning*. Teachers College Press.

Jewitt, C. (2006). *Technology, literacy, and learning: A multimodal approach*. Routledge.

Jewitt, C. (2008). Multimodality and literacy in school classrooms. *Review of Research in Education, 32*(1), 241–267. https://doi.org/10.3102/0091732X07310586

Johnston, E. (2025, November 24). Writing builds resilience by changing your brain. *The Conversation*. https://theconversation.com/writing-builds-resilience-by-changing-your-brain-helping-you-face-everyday-challenges-265188

Kahne, J., Hodgin, E., & Eidman-Aadahl, E. (2016). Redesigning civic education for the digital age: In pursuit of equitable and impactful democratic education. *Theory and Research in Social Education, 44*(1), 1–35.

Kress, G. (2010). *Multimodality: A social semiotic approach to contemporary communication*. Routledge.

Kwak, H., Lee, C., Park, H., & Moon, S. (2010). What is Twitter, a social network or a news media? In *International World Wide Web Conference Committee. Proceedings of the 19th International Conference on World Wide Web* (pp. 591–600). ACM. https://doi.org/10.1145/1772690.1772751

Lenhart, A., Arafeh, S., & Smith, A. (2008). *Writing, technology and teens*. Pew Internet and American Life. https://www.pewresearch.org/internet/2008/04/24/writing-technology-and-teens/

Lent, R., & Voigt, M. (2018). *Disciplinary literacy in action: How to create and sustain a school-wide culture of deep reading, writing, and thinking*. Corwin.

Lieberman, A., & Friedrich, L. (2010). *How teachers become leaders: Learning from practice and research*. Teachers College Press.

Lieberman, A., & Wood, D. (2002). *Inside the National Writing Project: Connecting network learning and classroom teaching*. Teachers College Press.

Maamuujav, U., Krishnan, J., & Collins, P. (2025). Multimodal writing: Affordances and rhetorical value of composing multimodally. In S. Graham, C. B. Olson, & T. Baker (Eds.), *Writing instruction across the disciplines: Evidence-based practices in grades (6–12)*. Routledge.

Mah, C., Walker, H., Phalen, L., Levine, S., Beck, S.W., & Pittman, J. (2024). Beyond cheatbots: Examining tensions in teachers' and students' perceptions of cheating and learning with ChatGPT. *Education Sciences, 14*, 500. https://doi.org/10.3390/educsci14050500

Mahdawi, A. (2025, January 8). AI-generated "slop" is slowly killing the internet, so why is nobody trying to stop it? *The Guardian*. https://www.theguardian.com/global/commentisfree/2025/jan/08/ai-generated-slop-slowly-killing-internet-nobody-trying-to-stop-it

Miller, M. (2023). *AI for educators*. Ditch That Textbook. https://ditchthattextbook.com/ai-edu/

Mills, K. A. (2010). A review of the "digital turn" in the new literacy studies. *Review of Educational Research, 80*(2), 246–271. https://doi.org/10.3102/0034654310364401

Muhammad, G. (2020). *Cultivating genius: An equity framework for culturally and historically responsive literacy*. Scholastic.

Murray, D. (1968). *A writer teaches writing: A practical method of teaching composition* . Houghton Mifflin Company.

Myhill, D. A., Jones, S. M., Lines, H., & Watson, A. (2011). Re-thinking grammar: The impact of embedded grammar teaching on students' writing. *Research Papers in Education, 27*(2), 139–166. https://doi.org/10.1080/02671522.2011.637640

National Council for the Social Studies (NCSS). (2013). *The College, Career, and Civic Life (C3) framework for social studies state standards*. National Council for the Social Studies

National Governors Association Center for Best Practices, & Council of Chief State School Officers. (2010). *Common Core State Standards for English language arts & literacy in history/social studies, science, and technical subjects*. http://www.corestandards.org/

National Writing Project et al. (2006). *Writing for a change: Boosting literacy and learning through social action*. Wiley.

National Writing Project, DeVoss, D., Eidman-Aadahl, E., & Hicks, T. (2010). *Because digital writing matters: Improving student writing in online and multimedia environments*. Jossey-Bass.

National Writing Project & Nagin, C. (2003). *Because writing matters: Improving student writing in our schools*. Jossey-Bass.

New London Group. (1996). A pedagogy of multiliteracies: Designing social futures. *Harvard Educational Review, 66*(1), 60–92.

Nystrand, M. (1986). *The structure of written communication: Studies in reciprocity between writers and readers*. Academic Press.

Organisation for Economic Co-operation and Development (OECD). (2019). *PISA 2018 results (Volume I): What students know and can do*. OECD Publishing. https://doi.org/10.1787/5f07c754-en

Ong, W. J. (2002). *Orality and literacy: The technologizing of the word*. Routledge.

Palmeri, J. (2012). *Remixing composition: A history of multimodal writing pedagogy*. Southern Illinois University Press.

Pew Research Center. (2025, September 25). *Social media and news fact sheet*. Author. https://www.pewresearch.org/journalism/fact-sheet/social-media-and-news-fact-sheet/

Rami, M. (2014). *Thrive: Five ways to (re)invigorate your teaching*. Heinemann.

Smith, M. W., Wilhelm, J. D., & Fredricksen, J. E. (2012). *Oh, yeah?!: Putting argument to work both in school and out*. Heinemann.

Smitherman, G. (1977). *Talkin and testifyin: The language of Black America*. Houghton-Mifflin.

Spear, K. (1986). *Sharing writing: Peer response groups in English classes*. Boynton/Cook.

Turner, K. H., Abrams, S. S., Katić, E., & Donovan, M. J. (2014). Demystifying digitalk: The what and why of the language teens use in digital writing. *Journal of Literacy Research, 46*(2), 157–193. https://doi.org/10.1177/1086296X14534061

Turner, K., & Pankiewicz, G. (2023). Developing writers in the new digital age: Ethical stances for writers and teachers. In Dehart, J. (Ed.), *Critical roles of digital citizenship and digital ethics* (pp.99–115). https://doi.org/10.4018/978-1-6684-8934-5.ch007

Vosoughi, S., Roy, D., & Aral, S. (2018). The spread of true and false news online. *Science, 359*(6380), 1146–1151. https://doi.org/10.1126/science.aap9559

Vygotsky, L. (1978). *Mind in society: The development of higher psychological processes*. Harvard University Press.

Wardle, C. (2020). *Understanding information disorder*. First Draft. https://firstdraftnews.org/long-form-article/understanding-information-disorder/

Wardle, C., & Derakhshan, H. (2017). *Information disorder: Toward an interdisciplinary framework for research and policy making. disinformation*. First Draft. https://firstdraftnews.org/long-form-article/understanding-information-disorder/

Wardle, E. (2007). Understanding "transfer" from FYC: Preliminary results of a longitudinal study. *WPA: Journal of the Council of Writing Program Administrators, 31*(1–2), 65–85.

Weaver, C. (1979). *Grammar for teachers: Perspectives and definitions*. National Council of Teachers of English.

WestEd. (2025). *Friction by design*. https://digitalfluency.wested.org/introduction-to-friction-by-design/

Whitney, A. (2020). Response: Talking back and forth between memory and Legacy in the National Writing Project. In N. Elliot & A. Horning (Eds.), *Talking back: Senior scholars and their colleagues deliberate the past, present, and future of writing studies* (pp. 83–84). Utah State University Press

Whitney, A. (2021). *Growing writers: Principles for high school writers and their teachers*. National Council of Teachers of English.

Whitney, A. E., & Friedrich, L. (2013). Orientations for the teaching of writing: A legacy of the National Writing Project. *Teachers College Record, 115*(7), 1–37. https://doi.org/10.1177/016146811311500707

Whitney, A., & Johnson, L. (2017). The persistent relevance of a writing process orientation. *English Journal, 106*(4), 82–25.

Whitney, A. E., McCracken, C., & Washell, D. (2019). *Teaching writers to reflect: Strategies for a more thoughtful writing workshop*. Heinemann.

Wolf, M. (2018). *Reader, come home: The reading brain in a digital world*. Harper.

Yancey, K. B. (1998). *Reflection in the writing classroom*. All Utah State University Press Publications. https://digitalcommons.usu.edu/usupress_pubs/120

Index

About the Authors

Kristen Hawley Turner is Professor and Chair of Education at Drew University in New Jersey. She is the founder and director of the Drew Writing Project and Digital Literacies Collaborative, and the author of numerous books and articles on the intersections between technology and literacy.

Tanya N. Baker is the executive director of the National Writing Project. She has worked as a high school English teacher, served as the director of the University of Maine Writing Project, and was for several years the director of National Programs at NWP.

Elyse Eidman-Aadahl, now retired, is executive director emerita of the National Writing Project. She was formerly a high school English and journalism teacher, faculty in the College of Education at Towson University, and director of the Maryland Writing Project. Her research focused on youth civic engagement, digital writing, and connected learning inside and outside of schools.

Tonya B. Perry is director and principal investigator for the Miles College Red Mountain Writing Project, and the provost and senior vice president at Miles College, an HBCU in Fairfield, Alabama. She is also a past president of the National Council of Teachers of English.